PRAISE FOR *WILL THE CIRCLE BE UNBROKEN*

"As the granddaughter of A. P. and Sara Carter and the great-niece of Maybelle and Ezra Carter, *Will the Circle be Unbroken* has had significant meaning to me as far back as I can remember. Both honored and exceedingly proud of the album, I knew what the Dirt Band did would forever change the way the world viewed the music I grew up with. That I should be writing this for my friend John, to pay tribute to the book he has written, celebrating the fiftieth anniversary of the album's release, with Bill's wonderful photos—many never before seen—is an honor and a humbling experience for me. I love John and all the 'Dirty Boys,' as Aunt Maybelle lovingly called them. They became part of the Carter Family when they entered the Woodland studio in August of 1971." —**Rita Jett Forrester**, Director, Carter Music Center, Inc.

"Thank you, brother John McEuen, for 'reacquainting' me with the Nitty Gritty Dirt Band's *Will the Circle Be Unbroken*. What an impact these recordings have had on American music! Revisiting the musical journey of the Dirt Band has reopened up my own life's musical influences and interests as a young boy growing up in households with parents and grandparents from Texas, Tennessee, Arkansas, and California. Along my path as a musician, artist, engineer and producer, I hear their influences. These musicians and performers continue to inspire me to play, sing, and write my own music."—**Jim Messina**, co-founder of Poco and Loggins & Messina, member of Buffalo Springfield

"*Will the Circle Be Unbroken* is one of the most important musical recordings ever made. It is the generational bridge between the genius of Earl Scruggs, Maybelle Carter, Roy Acuff, Merle Travis, Doc Watson, and Jimmy Martin and the delightful new exposure Vassar Clements, Norman Blake and Bashful Brother Oswald received in the rock and pop world. These recordings just keep helping traditional country and bluegrass music survive and furthering the dignity and importance of the musicians featured."—**Sam Bush**, American mandolinist, member of New Grass Revival, and International Bluegrass Music Hall of Fame inductee

"*Will the Circle Be Unbroken* is like a musical time machine. It takes me back to La Jolla, California, in the mid-1970s when I was learning to play banjo, cutting my teeth at bluegrass jams about one hundred miles south and fifteen years after the beginning of John McEuen's banjo journey. There's no telling how many times I listened to the *Circle* album, but when I revisit it now I realize that those tracks became a part of my musical DNA. Listening again to Earl and John's gorgeous double banjo rendition of 'Soldier's Joy,' I realize that I've spent most of my career trying to record a banjo duet as cool as that—and I'm still trying!"—**Alison Brown**, Grammy-winning American banjo player, guitarist, composer, and producer

"If one were to choose the most influential country record album of all time it would almost certainly be *Will the Circle Be Unbroken*. Fifty years later we now have this remarkable book, which not only chronicles how this pivotal moment came to be, but also fills out the saga with fascinating detail and backstory. Add to that the remarkable photographs—a great many never before published—which capture the interaction of these young men with the country music legends they so admired. *Will the Circle Be Unbroken* was, and is, a treasure. So is this book."—**Ranger Doug**, Harmony Ranch, co-founder of Riders in the Sky

"The *Will the Circle Be Unbroken* album was just as influential to my career as *Sgt. Pepper's*. I remember like it was yesterday as my band was riding through downtown Louisville, Kentucky, after a gig, hearing a cut from the album. The Dirt Band had found a way to bring to light this music for an audience that had been unaware of it for too long. I thank The Nitty Gritty Dirt Band and the *Circle* album for paving the road that I so happily traveled. The circle is infinite." —**T Michael Coleman**, bass player for Doc Watson

"*Will the Circle Be Unbroken* defied record store placard definition. Was it country, rock, popular? *The Circle* was all of those. Countless bands, young in 1972 or new in 2021, connect with the *Circle* album. Every listen, you return. Now with these rare photographs, you see this event unfold." —**Steve Martin**, radio host of "Unreal Bluegrass"

"Maybelle Carter, Earl Scruggs, Jimmy Martin, Doc Watson, Roy Acuff, Vassar Clements, Merle Travis, and more. The *Circle* album, actually a bountiful three-record set of informally brilliant music-making, was a seismic acoustic event, the Dirt Band's way of honoring their bluegrass and country heroes. It revived some careers and allowed the progenitors to reach a new and much wider audience. As someone on the festival scene in those early '70s, I saw the outdoor gatherings proliferate and found larger crowds to play for thanks to the vision of the Dirt Band and the willingness of their heroes to embrace a unique and unifying concept."—**Tony Trischka**, renowned banjo player, recording artist, and educator

"One of my most cherished bluegrass possessions—which hangs framed on my office wall at the International Bluegrass Music Association headquarters in Nashville—is a well-worn copy of the album *Will the Circle Be Unbroken*. The album had a significant impact on my musical and professional journey, without question. And it stands as a seminal work that was important in developing the International Bluegrass Music Association and the lives of our members."—**Pat Morris**, executive director of the International Bluegrass Music Association

"The *Circle* album was one of my very favorite albums ever recorded. It was absolutely magical from start to finish. I literally wore it out. The bass playing by Junior Husky and Ellis Padget formed much of the style I play today. I had to learn Padget's break on 'Lonesome Fiddle Blues' as soon as I heard it. This album may be one of the main reasons I got into the music business."—**Terry Smith**, three-time nominated and IBMA award–winning upright bass player for The Grascals

"For music fans who were ecstatic when they discovered the Nitty Gritty Dirt Band's *Will the Circle Be Unbroken* album in 1972, this book by John McEuen will be a real treasure. John fills us in on the making of *Will the Circle Be Unbroken*, from how he asked Earl Scruggs to be a part of the music project to stories from the studio. He also includes nearly a hundred never-before-seen photos from these 1971 recording sessions. John has done a great job in sharing more of its history, telling the story as only he can, from the memories of someone who was there when the idea for the album was born."—**Vernell Hackett**, music journalist and former editor of *American Songwriter* magazine who has written for *Billboard* magazine, *Country Weekly*, TheBoot.com, Reuters, and SoundsLikeNashville.com.

"The recording projects and the song "Will the Circle Be Unbroken" have been and continue to be a beautiful timeless centerpiece of country and bluegrass music. When I think of the many artists who contributed to both, it warms my heart as I remember it as a landmark project that displayed the ultimate camaraderie between artists and the talent that came together to create an historical album that continues to inspire fifty years after its creation."—**Rhonda Vincent**, American bluegrass singer, songwriter, and multi-instrumentalist

"This album affected virtually every string band musician, one way or another. Celebrating the prime movers of bluegrass and country music spotlit our heroes and their music, with benefits still coming to the whole community. The fellowship was palpable, a precious part of what naturally attracted a new generation of musicians worldwide—learning the songs, learning to pick. It sure helped me get banjo students, which led me to write an instruction book, which sold so well I quit my job and became a full-time musician. Still am! Thanks John, Earl, Doc, et al., and all the Nitty Gritties!"—**Peter Wernick**, Grammy-nominated banjo player, educator, and founder of Country Cooking and Hot Rize

"*Will The Circle Be Unbroken* was like getting handed American music on a silver platter. I listened to it a thousand times, and so did many of my musician friends. The duet on 'Soldier's Joy' introduced me to the possibilities of instrumental harmony in traditional music, which became a centerpiece of my life's work. Did this record influence me? *Hell yes!*"—**Michael Miles**, banjo player and educator at Old Town School of Folk Music

"Why do we love this album so much? Because it serves as a reminder to American souls and beyond of the tunes of our ancestors—songs that brought joy and happiness in hard, dark times, delivering Mother Maybelle Carter's lesson to "Keep on the Sunny Side" at the same time. A true salve when feeling lost or troubled, or joyful and hopeful. Real honest, raw, wonderful music just like the biscuits Mamaw made. You can live off this stuff, and even if you never heard anything else, you will feel full."—**Gracie Muldoon-Davis**, broadcaster and founder of Worldwide Bluegrass

"The *Circle* album set the stage for artists to collaborate with musicians from very different musical backgrounds and cultures. The Nitty Gritty Dirt Band proved that good music is good music. They made it possible to bring together musicians from all parts of the country, from all walks of life, and from all genres of music. And just as the Dirt Band brought diverse musicians together to make a great record while honoring each musician's traditions and unique talents, their music continues to bring people together."—**Wendy Tyner**, Wintergrass Festival, director of philanthropy/publicity, 2020 IBMA Mentor of the Year Award, 2018 CMA recipient

WILL THE CIRCLE BE UNBROKEN

The Making of a Landmark Album

JOHN McEUEN WITH PHOTOGRAPHS BY WILLIAM E. McEUEN
WITH STORIES BY THE NITTY GRITTY DIRT BAND AND GUEST CONTRIBUTORS
FOREWORD BY KEN BURNS AND DAYTON DUNCAN

Backbeat Books

Essex, Connecticut

Backbeat Books

An imprint of Globe Pequot, the trade division of
The Rowman & Littlefield Publishing Group, Inc.
4501 Forbes Blvd., Ste. 200
Lanham, MD 20706
www.rowman.com

Distributed by NATIONAL BOOK NETWORK

Library of Congress Cataloging-in-Publication Data

Names: McEuen, John, 1945– author.
Title: Will the circle be unbroken : the making of a landmark album, 50th
    anniversary / John McEuen.
Identifiers: LCCN 2022000239 (print) | LCCN 2022000240 (ebook) | ISBN
    9781493062331 (cloth) | ISBN 9781493062348 (ebook)
Subjects: LCSH: Nitty Gritty Dirt Band. Will the circle be unbroken. |
    Bluegrass music—1971-1980—History and criticism. | Country
    Music—1971-1980—History and criticism.
Classification: LCC ML421.N58 M34 2022 (print) | LCC ML421.N58
    (ebook) |
    DDC 782.421642092/2—dc23
LC record available at https://lccn.loc.gov/2022000239
LC ebook record available at https://lccn.loc.gov/2022000240

♾™   The paper used in this publication meets the minimum requirements
of American National Standard for Information Sciences—Permanence of
Paper for Printed Library Materials, ANSI/NISO Z39.48-1992

This book is dedicated to photographer William E. McEuen, a visionary in film, television, stage, and thankfully, records. He never wanted the spotlight himself, but I think he liked knowing, with his contributions, he deserved it.

Special thanks to William E. McEuen, for you made something as equally enduring as your favorite movie, *Citizen Kane*.

WILLIAM EUGENE McEUEN (A.K.A. BILL) 1941–2020

Artist Manager, Record Producer, Television Producer, Film Producer (Aspen Film Society), studio owner (Aspen Recording Society), multiple Grammy Award winner, Academy Award Nominee. William E. managed/produced the Nitty Gritty Dirt Band (records, TV, movies), Steve Martin (records, TV, movies), Pee-wee Herman (records, TV, movies), Steve Landesburg (records), Starwood (records), Stephen Wright (records, TV), Louisiana's Le Roux (records), Robert Schimmel (records, TV), The Sunshine Company (records, TV), Merrell Fankhauser (records), the early Allman Brothers (as The Hourglass—records), his brother John McEuen (records, film scores, TV), and several other acts in show business.

As a songwriter and guitarist, he was musical mentor to his brother, who was five years younger, teaching seventeen-year-old John McEuen guitar, guiding his career in the ensuing years—Bill came up with those magic chords to John's signature song, "Dismal Swamp."

Produced by William, the Nitty Gritty Dirt Band's 1972 *Will the Circle Be Unbroken* record—in the Library of Congress and Grammy Hall of Fame and the NGDB song "Mr. Bojangles" (also in Grammy Hall of Fame) alone would have been enough of an accomplishment for some producers other than Bill. Episode 6 of the PBS Ken Burns documentary *Country Music* was titled "Will the Circle Be Unbroken." John closed that episode with Bill's photos and the story of the making of *Will the Circle Be Unbroken* album.

But film called him. With Steve Martin's *The Jerk* and *Pee-Wee's Big Adventure* (two of nine films produced by Bill for his company, Aspen Film Society), comedy movies were never the same. Martin's four albums (produced/recorded live by Bill, who also designed the record covers) would do ten million units and change the comedy world. His production of Martin's iconic "King Tut" sold nearly two million units, hitting *Billboard*'s #2 spot.

Bill "made the deal" for NGDB being the first American band to go to Russia (1977, twenty-eight shows).

William E. was mentor to many who continue today in show business doing great things. He left behind a bunch of singing, laughing, and dancing people with happy feet who loved what he brought them. He *knew* what they would like! "Bill," a.k.a. William E. McEuen, has left the building.

For a complete list of his credits please go to https://www.imdb.com/name/nm0568530/ or https://en.wikipedia.org/wiki/William_E._McEuen.

GARY SCRUGGS 1949–2021

That Gary went to a record store, found our *Uncle Charlie* album, took it to his parents, played several songs, making sure the last song was Earl's *Randy Lynn Rag,* was clever. His vision was to have Earl record with us. We first met in the fall of 1970 when he drove his entire family to see us—Nitty Gritty Dirt Band—perform our first Nashville date.

He told me later when we opened and then encored with his dad's "Foggy Mountain Breakdown" that the whole family felt proud. Jamming backstage after the show led to developing a friendship, which allowed me to ask his dad, the following June while the Revue was working in Colorado, if he would record with this ragged bunch of hippies. Earl said "I'd be proud to." Thanks, Gary. I would become the first banjo picker to record with Earl!

This led to the making of *Will the Circle Be Unbroken*, and our friendship grew. Gary's vision to put us together led to a platinum record for all, putting everyone in the Grammy Hall of Fame, The Library of Congress, and became a part of so many lives—a record that we are forever indebted to Gary for initiating. Thank you, Gary.

He was always protective of his father, carefully managing things of music business, especially after the passing of his beloved mother, Louise. Earl and Louise made many of the necessary contacts for the *Circle* album, but Gary was our "ambassador" to the icons, keeping things running smooth.

A great chess player, we never could remember who was ahead, so we played again. It seems like the dinners, lunches, and "hanging out" were never enough. I will miss his smile and sheepish grin at a joke he would throw out, and his hearty laugh at one thrown to him.

Scheming with his mom, we got his song The Lowlands on *Circle III*, sung by my son Jonathan and Jeff's son Jaime. The Lowlands was absolutely great, one my brother, Bill, called "the Walk Away, Renee" of country music. It was the only song chosen by the record company for a music video, which landed the boys a major recording contract. Again, thank you, Gary.

When NGDB was recording in 2009. I told Gary to bring his best song to the studio . . . he brought over one, we listened in the car. His grin of confidence in the song was understood . . . I took it to the band, listening to songs. Jeff said he wanted do it! We ended up naming the album after his great song "Speed of Life." Thanks, Gary.

I will miss the times we were *always* laughing about something, not remembering exactly what. There were many. Sorry to see you go, my friend. You are missed. Rest in peace.

CONTENTS

FOREWORD

Fifty years ago, in summer 1971, a group of long-haired musicians from Southern California began setting up in the Woodland Studios of East Nashville, across the Cumberland River from fabled Music Row. The Nitty Gritty Dirt Band was not considered a "country" band, especially in Nashville, but they were about to make country music history.

John McEuen, the band's banjo player, had already persuaded his hero, the legendary Earl Scruggs, to take part. With Scruggs's help, they had recruited other legends in country and bluegrass music to join them. Among them were Doc Watson, Merle Travis, Jimmy Martin, and Mother Maybelle Carter (of the fabled Carter Family), whose landmark 1927 sessions in Bristol, Tennessee, had helped launch country music into the nation's consciousness. Bill Monroe, the "Father of Bluegrass," turned them down (and probably later regretted it). So did Roy Acuff at first, leery of the group's shoulder-length hair and suspicious of their intentions. But the fiddle prodigy Vassar Clements came along, as did Randy Scruggs, still in his teens, yet already recognized as an extraordinary guitarist.

As word spread about the sessions, many Music City insiders were perplexed by the project, wondering why a young group like the Dirt Band—hot off the national success of their rendition of Jerry Jeff Walker's "Mr. Bojangles"—would choose to make an album with so many "dinosaurs" of the industry backing them up.

But inside the Woodland studio, once the sessions began, it became clear that these West Coast hippies had no interest in having country and bluegrass artists accompany *them*; the Nitty Gritty Dirt Band wanted to back up the legends. Together, they started recording some classic songs that hadn't been widely popular in a generation.

William E. McEuen, John's older brother, was the producer (and, thankfully, found time to chronicle the moment by taking scores of photographs). He made a number of decisions that give *Will the Circle Be Unbroken* its unique sound. He arrayed the artists in a large circle, many of them in comfortable chairs facing each other—"like being at your home and just having a 'picking party,'" Randy Scruggs remembered. They recorded on a two-track tape, a seemingly quaint method compared with the four-track and eight-track methods most studios were using at the time. "We wanted to make an 'old' record," John McEuen said. "For us, it was like going back to 1928 and making early records." William also kept the tape rolling in between songs, capturing the banter between the musicians as they talked about their songs, their mutual admiration (Doc

Watson had named his son Merle in honor of Travis, his guitar hero, whom he was meeting for the first time), and how they would approach the next take.

The result was magical, allowing the listener to imagine he or she is sitting there, too, cozily surrounded by friends who just happen to be extraordinary musicians taking part in a "picking session" of historic proportions.

Near the end of the six-day session, Acuff—the "King of Country Music"—showed up, listened to what the group had already done, and decided to take the lead on some of the classics he had made famous from the stage of the Grand Ole Opry back in the 1940s.

On the title track, "Will the Circle Be Unbroken," everyone joined in, creating a timeless version of a timeless American song.

Looking back half a century, given *Circle*'s remarkable success and enduring place in recording history (the Library of Congress selected it for addition to the prestigious National Recording Registry), it's worth noting that on the three-disc album's initial release, it got little play on country radio. But some progressive FM stations started featuring it, and it caught on, especially on college campuses—spreading by word of mouth and helping to introduce a new generation to a quintessentially American art form.

The album's music will live forever. This book—with its extraordinary photographs—takes us behind the scenes to relive the historic moment when it was recorded.

Dayton Duncan

Ken Burns

ACKNOWLEDGMENTS

First, I need to thank William E. McEuen for his foresight, photography, design, and mixing/production skills, without whom this album would not have come together to create what he called "my masterpiece" (and, for the right rhythm guitar on "Honky Tonk Blues"). Two-track was right, too! And, to your wife Alice, whose painstaking work on the calligraphy was a perfect choice.

The other essential parts of this creation's credits then go to the NGDB, without whom we would not have had the music: Jimmie Fadden, Jim Ibbotson, Jeff Hanna, Les Thompson, and myself; we all came to the studio prepared to make this recording.

Thank you, Gary Scruggs, for enticing your dad to come see us the previous year (to recording) at that Vanderbilt concert. It sparked the idea in Earl (and Louise, his wife) of "maybe we should do something together." We did. Thank you, Earl, for saying "I'd be proud to . . ." when this young banjo picker asked you to record with NGDB seven months later . . . and the same thanks to Doc for saying "yes" a week later. Thanks owed to Chuck Morris, the club manager who booked them (Tulagi, in Boulder) and helped set up the Doc meeting.

Engineer Dino Lappas did his fine work getting the best sound and was prepared to capture the essential essence of Earl Scruggs, Doc Watson, Roy Acuff, Maybelle Carter, Vassar Clements, Jimmy Martin, Merle Travis, Junior Husky, Norman Blake, Pete "Bashful Brother Oswald" Kirby, all complemented by the occasional appearances of Randy, Gary, and Steve Scruggs; Ray Martin; Merle Watson; and Ellis Padgett.

Others to whom thanks is owed, the people who made it look great, the first being Dean Torrence (Kittyhawk Graphics) for his fine layout of artwork and getting Ivy Hill to do such a great print job of this Grammy-nominated classic cover. Mike Stewart (UA President), for believing in an idea he did not think would sell, but years later gladly admitted to being wrong!

Others of importance for various roles would be Chet Flippo (*Rolling Stone*), countless DJs and radio personnel who played this "bluegrass record," Martha Flippo, Mike Carr, Larry Murray, Betty Travis, Gloria Belle, and Alice.

And to those who spread the word that there was a record that "you need to hear" and talked about this for the past fifty years . . . thanks! It remains magic to listen to the sessions and the talk between songs (thanks again, Bill!) and this body of work that will never be equaled and have the same respect as the "*Dark Side of the Moon* of bluegrass."

Thank you to John Cerullo, Carol Flannery, Chris Chappell, Della Vaché, Laurel Myers, Barbara Claire, and the publishing team at Backbeat Books.

Special thanks need to go to a stranger I met on the internet in June 2020. Not from a dating service, he left a LinkedIn message asking "you need some help with publishing anything?" I was getting materials together with my brother in December (2019) for a "*Circle*-at-fifty" book, and I needed help. Bill had given me all the photos the previous year, and said "good luck," and left it in my hands to execute. I was glad he had faith in me for that. Through some emails, I found Denny Hayes. He "knew" me, my "solo" past, NGDB records, my brother's work, and was a "worshipper" of the *Circle* album! What could be more perfect than an agent who understood what I was selling?!

I called him after a few days and, after about thirty minutes, finding out that his love of music was right up there with the many great books he "orchestrated" or produced, I quit looking for an agent for this eclectic book "about bluegrass/folk music." I wanted him to help me find the right publisher, with similar respect for the music and photographs as I had.

While Denny made the "deal" as agent with the ideal publisher for our idea (Bill and me), he then jumped into the editing, logging, and making a road map of the production—things needed to bring it to fruition. I could not have handled all this; additionally, his previous experiences seemed to lead to doing it all for this book. Thank you, Denny Hayes! It seems like you were at the sessions, which is what I hope to accomplish for everyone with the stories and wonderful photographs of William E. McEuen.

INTRODUCTION

The path to the *Circle* album: a teenage dream comes true for many. This story is told by several participants and others around the event that became *Will the Circle Be Unbroken.*

The people include the members of the Nitty Gritty Dirt Band (NGDB): Jeff Hanna, Jim Ibbotson, Jimmie Fadden, Les Thompson, and John McEuen, who made it; Earl Scruggs and his wife Louise, who helped many come on board and make it happen, and most of those who participated who would rightfully call it "their" album. My brother Bill as producer was also photographer and cover designer; as it was recorded and brought home, he made it his masterpiece.

My story: Our father sold diesel equipment, and at fourteen years old, I had worked for him for twenty-five cents an hour, steam cleaning diesel parts, driving the forklift, and following Bill around like a puppy. By the time I hit fifteen, my salary had doubled! Although Bill played guitar a couple of years by then, I wasn't playing music yet but would be soon. My first "real" job was working in Disneyland at sixteen, the dream job of two teenagers (me and my high school friend, comedian Steve Martin) secured. We had just met in the spring of 1962. Disneyland was a great place to do magic tricks, sell them, and learn how to perform in front of an audience that would turnover every twenty to thirty minutes on a busy day, so if you weren't any good you could try again.

My "big brother" Bill didn't like tricks, but he was in love with Delta blues—Hank Williams, Stanley Brothers, Flatt & Scruggs, and other things that sounded strange and foreign to me, by "real" people, not showbiz stars. Well, except for Elvis. His fascination with and love of black blues made him wish he himself was black.

Bill also loved the film world and cameras—and tape recorders—and would get into various uses of those things as we were growing up.

Watching him play, me not playing as of yet, led to when I hit seventeen two years later and bought a Harmony guitar for $100 to try to play with him. He showed me things for about six months, but I could not play anything he did not know! My music came from Jimmy Reed, Freight Train, and some songs about a bank in Ohio through Bill . . . and I rushed a lot!

The summer of my seventeenth year came, and I needed something new. I mainly wanted to be close to him, get his "approval" (magic tricks did not do that) and things of that nature, and to do something together.

Steve and I had also been recently introduced to the banjo. We both saw Dave Simpson, the owner of a music store in Long Beach, playing banjo with my brother at my parents' house in 1963.

We were seventeen. Dave knew five songs—kind of—on the banjo. His "Jesse James" was killer! And he played the "Beverly Hillbillies Theme" right there in my living room! It was my first time up close and personal hearing a banjo, and it haunted me. The sound was fantastic. Steve felt the same way. We had to get banjos!

During this time living at home, working at Disneyland, going to Long Beach State College, Doc Watson appeared on Jack Linkletter's *Hootenanny* show doing "Deep River Blues." I sat watching, enthralled by him and his fingerpicking the guitar while singing, not knowing who he was. He sounded like three people. Captivated, I said out loud, "I want to meet him some day!" My father intoned, "Now, how a guy like that gets on TV, I don't understand." He did not hear what I was hearing: a way out of Orange County. . . . and evidence of the generation gap.

One night the next June, I let some friends drag me to a coffeehouse (Orange County's Paradox) to see a group I had never heard of, the Dillards. They came from Salem, Missouri, and they were tearing it up in Southern California clubs. That night, Doug Dillard's lightning banjo lit me and the whole room up!

I went home to my guitar, took off the fifth and sixth strings (as Rodney Dillard told me to do when I met him that night), put a first string where the fifth was, under an HO railroad spike at the fifth fret, and I had a "banjo"! I had to go see the Dillards the next night to find out how to tune it like a banjo. I wanted a banjo!

At seventeen and a half, with the banjo now in my life (I borrowed a Kay brand banjo for a while), all I wanted for my eighteenth birthday was my own banjo. My dad surprised me and bought my first real banjo for that birthday (arranged by brother Bill at the store run by Dave Simpson, a place that would mean so much to me—I had no idea—McCabe's Guitar Shop). I was on my way.

I became a college teenager with a car and a banjo, and a dream of *something*, but I just didn't know what. Seeing the Dillards two or three times a week, I practiced at home until midnight with records, in the car parking lot at college the next day, in the college practice rooms (between classes), and at McCabe's, which had become my new hangout. Wherever I could, I would pick. I was mesmerized by banjo! Nine months later, I was good enough to teach banjo at two different local music stores, making about a hundred dollars a week. After practicing eight to ten hours a day while in college, my second year I was ready to hit the stages in the area; it seemed like everybody was playing something! The folk music scene was in full swing.

Bill liked banjo, too, and he and I started learning some songs, with him on guitar and vocals and me on banjo. In those early two years, my big brother and I played a few clubs around Southern

California (calling ourselves the Fall River Tar Heels) as often as we could, including Golden Bear in Huntington Beach, the Troubadour's Hootenanny (Monday nights, run by Monkee-to-be Mike Nesmith), the Ash Grove in Hollywood, and a two-month gig at Sid's Blue Beet in Newport Beach. He sang Jimmy Martin, Hank Williams, Carter Family, and Dillards' songs (often, his wife Alice joined on harmony). We played Scruggs music and dreamed of the Grand Ole Opry. . . .

The following July, we convinced our father we should make a southern/mid-America trek, delivering and selling diesel things, taking care of some of his customers. Our secret intention was to get to the Grand Ole Opry . . . and it worked!

On a hot August Saturday night we made it to the Opry, but it was sold out! I went to the north windows, all open and raised up, to stare across the non-air-conditioned auditorium, at the stage. "Bill! Lester and Earl are on! They are going to play!" Right then, Lester Flatt said "Earl and I are gonna bring out Mama Maybelle Carter to do the "Wildwood Flar" [flower] for y'all." I almost passed out. I turned to Bill and said "I'm going to record with those people someday! I don't know how or when, but I've got to!" I needed a group, I figured.

Back home, hanging around McCabe's Guitar Shop, young Les Thompson (who was sixteen) and I started a bluegrass group that was a clone of the Dillards . . . kind of. We weren't very good, but the Wilmore City Moonshiners had a lot of energy. It lasted about a year, a couple dozen shows, and we broke up. (Before we quit, we opened for Hoyt Axton at the Golden Bear, a milestone for us.)

I then played banjo and guitar with local people at coffeehouses while in college: hootenanny nights, guest sets of four or five songs, not "real" jobs. I don't think I ever got paid. It was different back then, and people came to listen.

I played a few places with (my first girlfriend) Penny Nichols and folk artist (guitarist/singer) Mary McCaslin, and a few with new friend José Feliciano, a teenager from Puerto Rico—before he hit it big with "Light My Fire." Penny would end up on many albums and teach songwriting and singing in later years. Mary started her own career as a folk singer and did quite well. After a brief stint with Michael Murphey, I realized the Texas Twosome was not for me, because there were four of us, and I wasn't from Texas. (Many years later, when he added his middle name "Martin," I played on his hits "Wildfire," "Carolina in the Pines," and four of his albums.)

Then Les called and asked if I wanted to play with the guys at McCabe's, who I knew and picked with many times around the coffee table at McCabe's, and the Nitty Gritty Dirt Band was finally solidified. I taught them "Dismal Swamp," a tune I had written (with Bill), to back me up at the Topanga Canyon Banjo and Fiddle contest. Actually it was a playoff because of a tie, so

Bill and I played "Shuckin' the Corn" (an Earl Scruggs tune), and I won. Since I won, I decided to stay in the band.

A month later, I convinced my brother Bill, who was managing a band while going to film school, to "manage" the group. I did not really know what a manager did. We would find out.

Jeff Hanna and his high school classmate (and future NGDB member) Bruce Kunkel had a folk duo the New Coast Two. They later started a group called the Illegitimate Jug Band. That experience would serve them well in the Dirt Band's early years. Jimmie Fadden played great blues and funky harmonica with anyone, and he could play with anyone! Ralph Barr was the McCabe's fingerpicking guitar savant, and Les and I were from the Moonshiners. This would be the band that would make the first few albums, do PR photos, interviews, and with our first checking account, we were open for business! We played jug band music, a lot of songs learned from records made by Jim Kweskin, bluegrass, a few written by friends, songs from the 1920s and 1930s, all of which was the unusual repertoire of the band. Anything that we could, or wanted to, learn along the way was fair game. We were (as the reviews were saying) "a nascent group"; we showed potential . . . but for what?

Since I had first heard Jeff sing, his voice was different from those around, and his choice of songs was eclectic. I wanted to play with him. Jeff liked Ian and Sylvia and certain folk music and Jim Kweskin, and was good at all of it, and he was funny! Fadden was always willing to tackle anything: washtub, tuba, jug, guitar, mandolin but mainly focused on harp. Les on mandolin and bass and me with my banjo brought in mainly a bluegrass influence. None of us individually were as good as those whom we were emulating. But together, it was a unique combination. What made it work? "Why it worked" is something members of a band—any band—have trouble explaining, but it did. We all loved acoustic music. We were acoustic the first year or two . . . then things changed.

The band had formed, and we were under way. Bill would get us a record deal, even though he he was (we were) turned down by "every label in town" the first time. We would make hits, well, a one-hit run between 1966 and 1969. Bill landed us a couple of movies; we did television, played concerts and fairs; played with Jack Benny (four shows); opened for Little Richard for a month at Caesar's Palace in Las Vegas; and then later the Doors (East Coast shows) and then Bobby Sherman (a dozen shows on the East Coast, too). Bill shot a lot of photos, had great ideas, and went about finding a direction for us, and "things a manager does." I was learning he would do a lot.

This young Nitty Gritty Dirt Band would make four albums, do two movies, and a bunch of television shows, playing our version of jug band, folk rock, and the beginnings of country rock with a blend of bluegrass and folk thrown in, wearing pinstripe 1930s clothes usually picked up at

Goodwill. We all contributed something, and sometimes it wasn't easy, but good things were happening, like *The Tonight Show starring Johnny Carson*, *Rowan and Martin's Laugh-In*, *The Woody Woodbury Show*, *Dinah!*, local shows, and even a show hosted by a weatherman.

After filming *Paint Your Wagon* in 1968 for four months in Oregon's Walt Whitman forest with Lee Marvin, Clint Eastwood, Jean Seburg, and others, we broke up and went our separate ways. I didn't want to be in a band without Jeff in it, and Les didn't play bass yet, and it was time for something new.

Jeff went off to a band backing his friend Linda Ronstadt; Fadden and Les found jobs outside music; Chris Darrow went back to Claremont to teach; Ralph moved back in with his mother and taught guitar; and I played with others around town, did a few sessions, and then a month of Dobro, banjo, and guitar behind Andy Williams at Caesar's Palace (again) but this time in the main room!

I missed having a group. Even though the off-the-beaten-path music of NGDB was jug band and good-time music, it was fun. And "Buy for Me the Rain" (our first hit in 1967) had my disguised banjo on it (I had a mute on the bridge). The future looked brighter with a group (read this as "I thought we would possibly might have a chance to be maybe be successful . . . maybe").

Six months after we had disbanded, Jeff and I ran in to each other, watching Pogo in the Golden Bear, a place NGDB had played at least three times. They were killing it! (They later changed their name to Poco because of Walt Kelly's lawsuit.) We turned to each other and said, "let's get the band back together!" We agreed on doing that. He'd get Fadden; I'd contact Les . . . and he and I agreed that we needed a singing drummer.

The next day, Jeff saw Fadden, who had been working in a clothing store next to the Troubadour. He was in and out of the store in quick time. I called "happy about it" Les, who was working with his dad. Les was in. Then, Jeff and I went to meet a drummer who could sing and play. We made an "appointment" with Jim Ibbotson, up by where I lived in a duplex with Bill (my part of the rent was ninety dollars a month, utilities paid!). Jim was intimidated at first because he was from a place where "Buy for Me the Rain" had been played a lot. But, once he and Jeff sang together (Buddy Holly and other old rock and roll)—that was it for me, and Jeff, too—Jim was perfect.

The NGDB was together, with our "new guy" Jimmy Ibbotson (he likes to be called "Ibby"), Jeff Hanna, Jimmie Fadden, Les Thompson, and me. This was the second "birth" of the group. Ibby brought a whole new excitement and energy to the band, which was hard to define at times. He played drums and sang, played great rhythm guitar, bass, and piano a bit. He sometimes intimidated Jeff somewhat, but Jeff lived with it well. We all loved the energy we were creating.

We approached Bill to see if he would take us on again. He would! I did not want to be the guy who put the "tic" in eclectic and go without a manager. This second NGDB rehearsed in Long

Beach in 1969, down the street from McCabe's (Long Beach "branch" there at the time; the main McCabe's was in Santa Monica). With the heat of Vietnam getting hotter, but all of us "draft safe," we rehearsed for four and half months, six days a week. We were getting ready for something, not knowing what, other than to make an album, and we had to get better. With Bill going to produce now, a different type of record could be made. Maybe something with hits! We were still young. Bill got a deal for the "new" band with United Artists Records, and we kept rehearsing.

Produced by William E. McEuen (Bill), it was the first album with Ibbotson (our fifth album), an eclectic mix of tunes, to make our best and most successful album to date. Drums, electric guitars, bass, piano, accordion, harmonica, banjo, mandolin, acoustic guitars, washboard, washtub bass, and piano, and no rules. No title yet, but there would be—from one of those "inspirational moments" that came to Bill often. I still wanted to record with Earl Scruggs, someday. If we could get on the charts maybe that would be easier to do.

Before the NGDB came to be, Bill had recorded the uncle of his wife (Alice) in Tulare County, California. Her uncle, was a nice, funky old guy who played guitar, sang folksy songs, and blew the harp a bit. They would not sell him any more alcohol in his town. He and his dog were a pair. He could make his dog "sing" (howl) if he played the harmonica. It was a cool tape, and he filed it away for a couple of years. As he and I listened one night to the reference master of just finished final mixes of our "really good album," Bill said "go get the tape of the old guy with the dog and cue it up . . . up to when he gets the dog, Teddy, out from under the bed to sing." Bill, at the record player, had me start the tape—right *after* "Bojangles" ended. Hmmm . . . He said to play it again, and I did . . . this time with the man messing with his dog under the bed and blowing on a harmonica, prompting him to sing! Teddy, the dog starts to "sing" "The Old Rugged Cross" with Charlie . . . howling more with each prodding. Right then, as the dog howls, Bill drops the needle to start "Mr. Bojangles." We did it a couple of times. About midnight Bill called Dino, the engineer, and said "you have to meet me at the studio tomorrow morning. We have to remaster! . . . I have some editing to do. See you then."

The album had a concept brewing; soon it would be called *Uncle Charlie & His Dog Teddy*. Bill had photos of Charlie and used them on the cover. Charlie died a bit after Bill did the recording with him, from drinking too much hair tonic, so we were told.

Over the following year, it was starting to work! Our newest album, which now had a concept and title, would have three chart records on it! This mix of folk, good-time, pop/country rock, and bluegrass was the key to, the path to, the *Circle* album. We did "Randy Lynn Rag" and "Clinch Mt. Backstep," two bluegrass tunes, but with washboard and washtub bass. Fadden played the washtub, making it sound like an actual bass, to Ibby's rhythm guitar, with my banjo and Les's mandolin plowing through playing leads to Jeff's washboard.

We didn't know it then, but these tunes would appeal to Jimmy Martin, Doc Watson, and Earl Scruggs and the country rock/pop songs would appeal to their sons, Merle Watson, Gary and Randy Scruggs, Ray Martin (Jimmy's son), and to Jody Maphis (fifteen-year-old son of fantastic country guitar legend, Joe Maphis; Jody played drums with the Earl Scruggs Revue) . . . enough so . . . well, read on . . . the rest is "history."

With "House at Pooh Corner," "Some of Shelly's Blues," and "Mr. Bojangles" on *Uncle Charlie & His Dog Teddy*, we were on the road pretty heavy, doing 230 road days that year. We moved out of LA "without getting killed or caught," and all of us, about a month apart, transplanted to Colorado (Bill, who was first, went to Aspen).

In Denver, we teamed up with a new agency—Stone County—run by Lance Smith. Lance understood what we were trying to do and where we needed to be, and booked us a lot of college dates on this newly burgeoning college booking circuit, even putting us in the south in this time of *Easy Rider*, for the first time. Thanks to Lance, we had our first date in Nashville in fall 1970 to play at Vanderbilt University. It was exciting because there was now a chance to see Earl again. If I could get to the Opry, I might get to meet him!

Since our first road dates, I was also road manager. When we started, I was the only one old enough to rent a car! Now five years later, I did that and helped our new roadie, Gary Mullen, get the equipment around. I did the advance on the dates, and after booking rental car, hotels, and flights, we'd get there, set up, and play. Fadden often helped with the equipment, which was loaded in a Ryder truck at whatever airport we hit. For Vanderbilt, Fadden, Mullen, and I were there early. Bill had come along on this trip, too, also early. He had brought his Sony video recorder with him to capture things. Was there anything to capture? Not yet. But it was Nashville.

As we were setting up in the gym, various students on the concert crew kept saying "hey, I heard Earl Scruggs is coming tonight." "I hear the Scruggs family will be here." Fat chance, slim chance I thought and went to the dressing room (girls' locker room!) to warm up. Putting my banjo slightly out of tune, I started playing "Foggy Mountain Breakdown," poorly and out of tune like a deaf beginner, as a joke for Bill. I went to answer a knock at the door, while I was still playing.

There stood the entire Scruggs family, Earl at the front, quietly grinning. I said, "Oh, shit!" and closed the door, with them all still outside. Earl asked through the closed door "Can we come in?" I let them in, embarrassed about the playing, and shocked it was Earl himself! I was excited! What a shock; I had to hear him pick. Telling him I was embarrassed about what happened and asked him if he would play "Fireball Mail" on my banjo (one of my favorite banjo tunes). Before I finished my question, he was getting banjo picks out of his pocket. Randy and Gary played along with him—it was great.

When it ended, I asked Earl why he had come to see NGDB. He said, "I wanted to meet the boy who played 'Randy Lynn Rag' the way I intended to." He floored me with that. It was his song, and he'd played with fire on a Flatt & Scruggs record, where I had learned it. I then played it, with a different fire, Gary on bass (he was a student at Vanderbilt at the time) and Randy on guitar. It was great playing with their timing. This all ended very amicably, with Earl leaving the room saying to us, "We should record together sometime." I would not see him again until seven months later in Denver.

"Mr. Bojangles" was getting huge in 1970, after the other two songs had paved the way. The NGDB was making money, officially "in the business," on the radio, and things were fine.

Five months later Doc Watson was playing in the LA area. I went to see him, wanting to meet him. It was too crowded, but I met his son Merle, explaining to him I had a plan: to ask Earl, a few months later, if he would record with NGDB. If he said "yes," then I wanted to meet and ask Doc, booked at the same club the week after Earl, the same question. He was excited about that possibility. I said "wish me luck," and bade him farewell.

The following June, the Earl Scruggs Revue was playing their five-night run in the Boulder club, Tulagi. Now a Colorado resident, I went to see him every night and, after the show, drove him to his hotel. We were getting to know each other a bit. His last night I got up my nerve and asked if he would record with NGDB, to which he said, "I'd be proud to!" Jeff was in the back seat, and I can still remember looking back at him and seeing his eyes bulging, with eyebrows up!

A week later, I ran up to Merle on Doc's night at Tulagi's and told him "Earl said 'yes'! You have to introduce me to your father!" He was excited, agreed, and took me to meet Doc, on the way saying, "This would be perfect—this folk music thing is dying out . . . the crowds are gettin' smaller." I met his dad and rambled about what we were thinking of doing, kind of like writing a term paper from the information in the library's card catalog. I told him I wanted to put him on the phone with the producer, my brother, to talk about it. Doc said "yes," and after their chat, we were under way!

Later on in this book, I will describe how that happened in more detail, but right now it is good to explain the excitement Bill and I had for this recording to happen. Earl Scruggs and Doc Watson—two of America's musical giants were going to record with us! Bill would mention Merle Travis the next day . . . and then said, "Roy Acuff said in an interview he would make REAL Country

Music with anyone, anywhere, anytime. I'm going to find out if he meant it. And Merle Travis would be good to include."

This would lead to a call to Wesley Rose, president of Acuff/Rose Music, one of the biggest publishing houses in Nashville. He would convince Roy. "Behind the scenes" Earl was working on his agenda because he and his wife Louise were a necessary part of all this happening. By the second and third weeks, Merle Travis was on board, a meeting with Roy Acuff was scheduled thanks to Earl, Maybelle Carter committed thanks to Earl and Louise, fiddle and bass players found (Earl had not told us yet), and we told the rest of the band of what was coming together. Another two weeks and all players would be lined up, and three or so weeks later we had to be in Nashville to rehearse!

Bill would make the cover of *Circle* come alive as we progressed. We made *Circle* with the intention of it being successful, taking the chance that our hits would continue afterward. It took a few years to recuperate on "hit radio," but FM did well for us. Basically, we all went out on a limb for the idea of recording great songs with great people: What could go wrong? What could go right?

In 2019, episode 6 of Ken Burns country music documentary was called "Will the Circle Be Unbroken"; where Jeff and I closed out that episode's last twenty minutes, using some photos from Bill, in this "book meant to be." The *Circle* remains unbroken.

"THE NITTY GRITTY CIRCLE"
THE BAND MEMBERS WHO PLAYED ON THE *CIRCLE* ALBUM

Jeff Hanna

When I was asked to write about *Will the Circle Be Unbroken*, it seemed a daunting task. Looking back down the road fifty years, through the fog of time—lots of memories to sift through. John suggested putting the record on the turntable and looking at his brother Bill's wonderful photographs from those sessions. Well, that did the trick. My apologies in advance for jumping around in time. It's just how my mind works. And as Earl Scruggs liked to say, "But, anyway. . ." It may have seemed a stretch to some folks when this scruffy rock band from the West Coast decided to go to Nashville and make a record with a group of older, perhaps more conservative, musical icons.

Preconceptions can be tricky. If you peeled back our band's history a bit, you would find an all-acoustic jug band, playing traditional, old-timey American music. And a few years prior, before there was a Nitty Gritty Dirt Band, we were all what I like to refer to as "folk puppies." Teenagers

Jeff Hanna PHOTO COURTESY JIM McGUIRE

in constant search of authentic, traditional roots music—The Holy Grail; the Real Deal. People like the Carter Family, Earl Scruggs, and Doc Watson. Is it starting to make sense?

In fall 1970, we were on an extensive tour of the South, playing mostly college campuses. A Vanderbilt University student named Gary Scruggs had become a fan of the Dirt Band, and when we played that show in Nashville, he'd arranged for he and his family to meet our band. That became a pivotal night in our history. From the moment we met Gary and his parents, banjo legend Earl Scruggs and his wife Louise, along with his brothers Randy and Steve, there was an immediate connection. It just felt like family to all of us. It should be pointed out, that the rock and roll from our *Uncle Charlie* album may have gotten the Scruggs boys in the door, but it was our version of the Earl Scruggs instrumental "Randy Lynn Rag," featuring John McEuen's incendiary, super-charged 5-string banjo, that really set the hook for Earl. He was duly impressed by John's playing and told him so. John was blown away, and we were all proud of that moment. We spent a good bit of time that night talking with the Scruggs family and playing a little music as well. On his way out the door, Earl mentioned that he'd love to record with us sometime—unbelievable. Here's where the story gets interesting.

A few months later, we each got a call from our manager and record producer Bill McEuen. He'd been with us in Nashville when we met the Scruggs family and had a brilliant idea. What if we took Earl up on his offer to record with us but expanded the concept to include a number of other artists from the folk and roots realm that we all admired and had been influenced by? Doc Watson and our old friend Merle Travis's names came up immediately. Bill mentioned Roy Acuff and maybe Bill Monroe, as well.

We'd relocated from LA to Colorado in spring 1971. That June, the Earl Scruggs Revue was playing in Boulder at a club we frequented, so we set out see them with a purpose. After the show John asked Earl if he'd still like to record with us. He said, "I'd be proud to." And we were off! John asked Doc Watson the same question a week or two later, and he signed on as well. It sure didn't hurt having Earl as an incentive, and . . . Doc's son Merle was a fan of ours too, just like the Scruggs boys were.

We met up in Nashville near the end of July. The plan was to rehearse with the Scruggses at their home in Madison and get to know some of the other players as well. Earl had brought in fiddler Vassar Clements to play on the record. Vassar had an extensive bluegrass background, but he could play pretty much any kind of music with authority—what an extraordinary musician and a great guy as well. Vassar was the first big surprise. The other one was Jimmy Martin.

Jimmy Martin was a revelation. Prior to meeting Jimmy and recording with him, I wasn't familiar with his music. But as it turned out, I'd been hearing his stuff for years when Bill and John would jam out to "Hold Whatcha Got." I loved that tune but had no idea who the artist was. That all changed when Bill Monroe declined to take part in the *Circle* project. He stated that he didn't think his fans would understand or approve. After the "Father of Bluegrass" passed on us, Earl and Louise Scruggs suggested that we give the "King of Bluegrass," Jimmy Martin, a try. Well now, that sure worked out. After a few days rehearsing with Vassar and the Scruggs family, it was suggested that we head over to Jimmy's house and get to work on becoming honorary "Sunny Mountain Boys." That became a crash course and master class in bluegrass harmony for the singers in the band and a high-speed tutorial and obstacle course for the pickers. Fortunately, John was a real student and devotee of Jimmy's former banjo player, the great J. D. Crowe, which helped a lot.

I should point out right here, that we were having a ball. Jimmy was a fine teacher, a real "detail guy" but patient and encouraging as well. A couple hours of picking and singing later, Jimmy said, "Y'all hungry?" He'd planned a little barbecue with some "surprises" for us. So, we all sat down to a beautiful spread. Mmmmm, Southern cookin'. After a few bites, Jimmy asked, "You boys like possum?" We immediately froze above our plates . . . "cuz you're-a-eatin, it!" Well, that particular varmint delicacy was not gonna happen with these California dudes. Right then he leaned back with a huge grin on his face. "Ha! I gotcha! It's just chicken, boys! eat up!" We all breathed a sigh of relief and laughed our asses off.

By the time the sessions began, we'd hit a good groove. We were ready. We convened at Woodland Sound Studios in East Nashville. Also joining us there were session ace Junior Huskey on bass and renowned acoustic musician Norman Blake on Dobro. I believe we got things rolling with Merle Travis, our old friend from the Ash Grove folk club days in LA. Merle had this cool, conversational singing style that really drew you in; he was a great songwriter, as well. And his guitar playing was flawless and innovative. "Travis Picking" . . . yep, that guy. After hearing those Travis tracks, Roy Acuff agreed to join us. He brought along his old sidekick from the Smoky Mountain Boys, Pete "Oswald" Kirby. Roy just sang his heart out. Pure mountain soul . . . and Oswald's Dobro playing provided the perfect counterpoint.

And Doc Watson . . . Doc loomed large in my world because I'd been a fan of his astounding guitar work and singing since I was a kid. Leaning over his shoulder and adding harmony on "Tennessee Stud" was an unforgettable moment for me. There were lots of those, believe me. Mother Maybelle Carter had been my first guitar hero, and sitting on the floor in front of her, watching her play "Keep on the Sunny Side" on her Gibson L-5 was priceless. She had this lovely serenity about her as well. Jimmy Martin just blew the doors off the place. He brought a whole lotta rock-and-roll energy with his high-voltage delivery. Jimmy was a great singer and could drive a band like a locomotive with his Martin D-28 guitar.

Meanwhile, we were tearing it up on Earl's instrumentals. Those tracks just killed me. Earl revolutionized the 5-string banjo. It's called "Scruggs style" for good reason, and he always made it look effortless. "Flint Hill Special" and "Nashville Blues" were two of my favorites. Eighteen-year-old Randy Scruggs's blazing guitar solos just knocked me out, and Vassar was just mind-blowing on that fiddle. I was so proud of my bandmates on those tracks. I think being in that room with our heroes really upped our game. We were operating on a combination of fear, anxiety, and joy, fueled by a ton of adrenaline. We just rode that wave, and it was a beautiful thing. Les's mandolin,

Jimmie's harp, and of course, Johnny's banjo were all truly inspired. Ibby and I held down the rest of it on either snare drum, guitar, or washboard most of the time.

On the singing side of things, we got to do a lot of harmony work. Ibby, Les, and myself, along with Gary Scruggs and Ray Martin, provided most of the background vocals on the record. There were some solo turns as well. Ibby's version of the Hank Williams classic "Lost Highway" was a real highlight; he just nailed it. And Jimmie Fadden's take on Hank's "Honky Tonkin'" was cool as can be. I sang "Honky Tonk Blues" and really enjoyed sharing lead vocals with Gary Scruggs on the Carter Family gem "You Are My Flower." John McEuen's instrumental "Togary Mountain" was terrific. Fine picking by all. And John and Earl's banjo duet on "Soldier's Joy" was absolutely stunning. We made some real magic within the walls of the Woodland Studio. What an honor it was to be in the same room with those musical giants. Their generosity of spirit carried us through. What might have been a great divide, musically and culturally, never materialized. Music won the day.

Finally, we all gathered to sing "Will the Circle Be Unbroken." The week had just flown by in a joyous blur. Was that a dream? Yes, it was. But it really happened. It took a village to make that record. Earl Scruggs jump-started it. Louise Scruggs worked tirelessly opening doors for us in the Nashville music community, and Bill McEuen's creative vision brought it all home.

Farther along listening to this record today reminds me of how grateful I am for the friendships that began all those years ago. We continued to make music with many of the artists on *Circle*. Later, when we decided to revisit *Will the Circle Be Unbroken*, Randy Scruggs became our producer. He did a masterful job on *Circle vol. 2 and vol. 3*. Those albums provided a great opportunity to reunite with some of our old friends from summer 1971. Earl and Randy Scruggs, Vassar Clements, and Jimmy Martin returned for both records. Doc joined us on volume 3, as well. But again, it was the friendships that endured. I'll never forget the Earl Scruggs "Birthday/Picking Parties" that Louise and Earl would host at their home on Franklin Road in Nashville. Catching up with them, Randy, Vassar, Pete Kirby. I miss all those folks so much. What great memories.

One more story before I go. My friend Dave Ferguson called me back in April 2005 and said "Jimmy's Martin's really sick. We should go see him." So we drove out to Jimmy's home outside Nashville. They'd set up a hospital bed in his living room, and Jimmy, who was pretty frail but in good spirits, was holding court. Soon as he saw me, he shouted from across the room, "Hey Little Jeff (his nickname for me) . . . good to see ya!" I was glad to see Jimmy, too. We sat and talked for quite some time. Had some big laughs as well. It was a good visit, but I could see he was getting tired and needed his rest. As I was getting up to head home, someone suggested that we sing a tune together. Jimmy lit right up. I grabbed his guitar and started to hand it to him, but he said I should play it. His hands were too weak. So I started to strum the chords to one of the songs we'd recorded together, "Losin' You (Might Be the Best Thing Yet)." I hadn't played but a few bars when Jimmy said, "Wait a minute! You ain't-a-pickin' that right! Ya gotta dig in with that right hand." I handed him the guitar, and he demonstrated the proper picking technique for me, Jimmy Martin Style . . . right back to 1971. Teacher and student. So I tried it again . . . another strum. He clapped his hands together and said, "There ya go! Now yer-a-gittin'-it!" We finished the lesson and the tune. Smiles and tears all around.

—JH

Jimmie Fadden

We were a bunch of sixties self-styled musicians in search of all things folk music. In its various forms and styles, we each had our favorites.: Appalachian, bluegrass, folk, blues. You name it, we loved it. As a group we didn't seem to be interested in anything too modern. And in the beginning we played strictly acoustic. Jug band music was a mainstay, and we had a banjo player so a couple of bluegrass instrumentals and one by Earl Scruggs fit right in. My harmonica playing seemed to blend with a variety of styles; my main influence was Sonny Terry, who had listened to the harp playing of DeFord Bailey on *Grand Ole Opry*. And the mandolin, well it had a much bigger future than we knew at the time. The guitar playing in the band was influenced by many greats including the finger style of Merle Travis whom we were fortunate enough to work with at the Ash Grove in 1967, and there was Doc Watson, whose "Black Mountain Rag" was a "flat-pickin" rite of passage. I guess you could say we were interested in the musical expression of rural America to be the foundation of our creativity.

Well at some point, I think our friends would have sworn that we had made a pact with Devil. What can I say, we had plugged in! Well not all the way in, ya' see, just part of the way in. We started combining electric and acoustic instruments, and I think that we felt that if we could contemporize the traditional forms that we had been playing, we might create something of our own. And so it was that by the time we got to the *Uncle Charlie* album, this crazy idea was making a lot of sense with us and had spawned cuts that were getting some attention at radio. Michael Nesmith's "Some of Shelly's Blues" with an intro featuring frailing banjo and harmonica intro and Kenny Loggins's "House at Pooh Corner" with my lead acoustic guitar coupled to a wah-wah pedal.

And here's where the mandolin becomes important, as previously mentioned, setting the mood right up front on Jerry Jeff Walkers "Mr. Bojangles." Now one important track to remember from

Jimmie Fadden PHOTO COURTESY RICK MALKIN

that album, a barn-burning Earl Scruggs instrumental "Randy Lynn Rag," named for Earl's second son Randy. So where is all of this going? Well Gary, Earl's oldest son, had been listening to the *Uncle Charlie* album and played it for his dad, who had high praise for John's banjo playing and our eclectic arrangement. Not only that, as it turned out, Gary was a student at Vanderbilt University, where we would play and where we would meet Earl and the family for the first time.

What a great surprise we had backstage after the show. Pickin', singin', an' tradin' stories, and discussing all things music. It felt like we had found a new circle of friends. It is from that night that an idea was born. A short time after Jeff and John went to see the Earl Scruggs Revue at the club Tulagi in Boulder, Colorado, and as I hear it, there, after the show it was reunion of kindred spirits not unlike that night in Nashville. It was John (with passenger Jeff) who drove Earl back to his hotel later, and in the car, John asked Earl if he would consider recording with us! And now this is going somewhere.

Next week at the same club John goes to see Doc Watson and proposes the same idea. With son Merle's enthusiasm as the catalyst, Doc agrees. Now, this is really going somewhere. I know that was a bit of a crazy explanation about how this all got started, but the pieces all have places . . . and that's the Dirt Band Way.

Bill McEuen, or William E., our manager, producer, and director of all things artistic, had a vision of something that we may not have guessed at. Something much larger than we might have considered. He called us all up and suggested that we get together and talk; he really believed this could work. He went to Liberty Records and came back with their blessing and a budget. We were going to Nashville to make a record. Now we are really, really going somewhere. I don't believe that all of what took place was part of the plan, as much as it was allowed to occur. From the moment that we arrived the project took on a life of its own. Bill had a great eye for developing opportunities.

Rehearsal at the Scruggs home in Madison, Tennessee, was music central; we were jamming in the backyard. We couldn't get enough music; this was great fun. We were becoming fast friends. Long, lost like-minded souls. This really put us at ease and set the mood for things to come. Here's where the hidden talent enters the picture: Louise Scruggs. She was, as we were to find out, a force of nature. She was the organizational talent, the person behind the curtain, suggesting additional artists, scheduling time to rehearse with others, always on the phone, and then making sure we all were fed, all the while adding possibilities to Bill's vision and, ultimately, the outcome of the *Circle*—our den mother extraordinaire!

I think our meeting with Merle Travis was next. This was special. As mentioned previously, we had played with Merle in California a few years before, so it was sort of a reunion at his house. There was a lot of warmth, a lot of talk about recording, and of course, the famous Bixby guitar on the wall. Then it was time to get to work, and as we got ready to play, he seemed a little hesitant about getting started. He told us that he in fact hadn't been playing much lately and felt rusty, hmm. We looked at each other, uh-oh! He pulled out his guitar, opened the case, it really was out of tune, mmm, not good—started to play—and fumbled a couple of licks. Really uh-oh! He stopped—looked around the room at all of us, dead silence—and then lit into "Cannonball Rag" just as fast and smooth as could be looking around the room at all of us, and damn, just smiling big . . . yah, big! We had been had by the man from Rosewood, Kentucky.

Now that the rules on good-natured pranks had been established, things are moving along. Next on the lineup was Jimmy Martin, a man with an unknown to us reputation for his wacky humor and wild ways. We were going to his house in Hendersonville. There was going to be a BBQ and, of course, plenty of bluegrass. Jimmy's passion beside music was hunting, and he loved his huntin' dogs' and doted on them—every one of them. He was such a character, never a dull moment.

"Now don't sing it like that, sing it like this. Let's do it again." Jeff, Les, and Ibby were getting the harmony parts together for "Sunny Side of the Mountain." Rehearsing at Jimmy's. I asked his son, Ray Martin, how he liked being on the road with his dad, "Done a lot of livin', done a lot of lovin'." The Bluegrass way of life; gotta love it! They would never understand that in California; just as well.

During this time there was, believe it or not, some time to kill, when the music had stopped, and we were done for the day. So, Randy, Gary and Stevie Scruggs, and Jody Maphis (a member of the Earl Scruggs Revue and son of country music stars Joe and Rose Lee Maphis) volunteered to entertain us. That, more often than not, led to a long Ping-Pong challenge at Joe and Rose Lee's house, with Jody left in charge. It's good when your parents are on tour. The champs for the week were John, Jody, and our friend and fellow banjo player, Steve Martin, who was along to witness one heck of a 5-string collaboration. You know, I have no idea who the ultimate winner was.

Woodland Sound studio was comfortable but not super snazzy, like some trying to bill you more for the decor than the equipment or sound. We knew if Dino Lapis, our engineer, was comfortable, everything would be just fine. We settled in and got to work. A collection of microphones surrounded by a circle of chairs greeted us. We had our places from where we could best hear and watch each other. This was live music, spontaneous play, working from our own notes about who did what and when.

Vocal parts, solo sequences, and our own ideas and information to create a chart to "git 'er done." Sometimes tunes were arranged on the spot. That's the beauty of this music: It is built for impromptu play; there's no sheet music, folks. It's all committed to memory, and that memory is constantly evolving. What you give is what you get, and there's no taking it back. The sheer thrill of what we jokingly refer to as "playing without a net." That's live to two-track recording No overdubs, no fixes, and no "coulda, woulda, shoulda."

Roy Acuff had a great moment where he shared his policy in the studio; he said that every time you went through it you would lose a little something. "So let's do it the first time an' t' hell with rest of it."

Coming into this project I had to wonder just how as a harmonica player I was going to fit in on some of the tunes. The horses' hooves on the gravel on "Tennessee Stud" were a good fit, but the really fast bluegrass was always a challenge. Well, meeting up with Vassar Clements, fiddle player extraordinaire, that question had an interesting answer. During rehearsals I found that there were melodic ideas that he would interject into his solos that I could provide a harmony part for or play along with. Our solos together were something some people have cited as completely original. I'm not sure about that, but we had fun with it.

It is hard to express what that experience has meant to me. There is the wonder of meeting and playing with people that you have always admired and will always admire. And then, sharing the influence that they have had on your life and music with others. There are the friendships that develop sharing the time together. Jeff and Jimmy Martin remained lifelong friends. He and I both moved to Nashville sometime thereafter. There are so many life changes for us that it accounts for. Not to mention the response from those who have listened to and found the joy that we had in making it; they are the audience and the true testament to the success of our effort. And they continue to share that joy with us. I know that music is alive and always will be, and I am so fortunate to have had a chair in that circle

William E. McEuen had a lot more in mind for this record than most of us, and we are all rewarded for that. I have always admired his ideas in all things recording and art. He, along with graphic artist Dean Torrence, were the kings of great album art; their work was always of the highest quality. I wanted to acknowledge Bill's wife, Alice McEuen. for all the hard work she put into the handwritten titles and credits on *Circle*, I don't think anybody knows what an undertaking that was. No computers back then, folks; make a mistake, start over. Just like two-track. I find it truly satisfying that people will have the chance in the fiftieth year of this album to see the session photos that Bill captured. He was such a great photographer, with his trusty Nikon always handy. How he managed the sessions and captured all the images for the album is beyond me

So, after that memory disclaimer in the beginning. Well, I don't know how much I have forgotten, or how much I still remember, but there is one moment that I really enjoy revisiting. One day during a little break, I was talking to "upright" bass player Junior Husky about his instrument. He had already admitted that he had a thing for "those ole Kay basses." In fact, someone had brought a second one to the studio that morning, presumably to determine whether one sounded better that the other. So, I asked him if he had others. "Oh yes" he said, "but I've got them all loaned out, like Harold Bradley with his guitars, and if they all came home at once my wife would divorce me!" Chuckle. So, we are standing there for a moment, and he then looks down, and for whatever reason, there is maraca sitting there on a music stand. He reaches down, picks it up, and examines it with a look of curiosity and then shakes it vigorously a couple of times, looks at me, and says, "I think there's something loose in there."

A good time was had by all, and I will never forget that.

I have to say right from the get-go that I am not in possession of a great memory. Whole tracks of time lost and out of reach, and there are those that will attest to this. So, if some of this is a little off or slightly inaccurate, so be it. This is fifty years ago in Dirt Band time that we are talking about here, and a lot of notes have gone under that bridge.

—JF

Les Thompson

One of the greatest moments in my involvement with the Nitty Gritty Dirt Band was the recording sessions for the *Circle* album. Aside from being part of a moment in time that will have repercussions for eons, it was an honor to perform with the musicians that were responsible for me ever wanting to play music in the first place. How often can a professional musician say, "this music idol's art was responsible for my life as a musician?" and then actually be able to perform with those artists and make a wonderful piece of art that will last forever? The *Circle* sessions will always be in the forefront of all the recordings the Dirt Band made together.

Les Thompson

It was interesting how it all evolved around John's ability to use the Dirt Band's past successful recordings to explain our roots. That each of the artists that were asked became an integral part of our musical development. It was a perfect project for our appreciation of what they (Mother Maybelle, Doc, and the rest of our musical idols) gave to the band in honoring their musical heritage.

The sessions themselves were a bit of a white-knuckle experience for myself. Not speaking for the rest of the band, but I was terrified in the beginning. (I just didn't know it.) I always was a little keyed up and thought it was just nerves. But in the end, it was a bit of stage fright. Sitting with these musical giants, talking about each tune and figuring out the arrangements were all spur of the moment. "Let's do this tune. John and Earl will take banjo breaks, Earl will kick it off, Vassar will take the second break, Les takes the third break, John will take the fourth, Earl will bring it home." For me, some of the tunes were familiar, but all in all, we did not tell anyone what tunes we were going to do.

It all evolved out of what each musician wanted to do, and of course, the hits that each one brought to the table. I have to say that of all the musicians that participated in the session the one musician that did not wish to be a part of the project was Bill Monroe. That was in retrospect a blessing for me because I played most of the mandolin in these sessions. It put me in a prominent role in the music. That made John and I sitting in all the instrumental tunes except when I would be singing with Jeff, Ibby, or Jimmy, singing back up or leads on a few of the tunes.

I did not play bass because we had one of the best bass players of all time, Junior Husky. The fact that Bill Monroe did not participate made it easy for me to fill my own shoes. There are so many memories and stories that can be conveyed during those sessions; one could go on and on.

After the sessions we would go back to the hotel and decompress with friends and other Nashville musicians who heard about the sessions and wanted to know how they went. Sitting with Earl and Vassar in those sessions will never ever be forgotten.

I remember the first day of recording. I told Vassar how nervous I was about the tunes and not being able to rehearse any of them together. (Vassar and I became close the month preceding the sessions, so I was not too closemouth about how nervous I was.) I told him when we all entered the studio that I was having a white-knuckle moment, and he said, "Let's sit next to each other and all you have to do is follow my lead when you don't know a tune, and you will be just fine!" I have to say, that if it wasn't for that I would probably would have had musician's block. He really saved the day for me. Our friendship lasted for years, and whenever he came to my region to perform, he always told me and asked me to join him on stage. I will always cherish his friendship and his genuine sincerity in helping me with those sessions.

The Dirt Band was a highlight of my life, and like all bands, we had our ups and downs. Personality bumps and differences of opinions were no different from most other bands. I regret that I left the band in the end, and it was not easy, but we all adjust and make our way through those times. It did open up some avenues for me, and I did not do too bad after musical years. I was able to make an admirable living writing commercials for a number of years. I did a few soundtracks for television shows including ABC's *After School Playbreaks*. (Unless you're old as dirt, you won't know what I am talking about!) I often think back and fondly remember different musicians I have been lucky enough to perform with, rub elbows, and tell stories. I have been fortunate to have been a founding member of the Nitty Gritty Dirt Band and to contribute what I could during those formative years of the band.

—Les Thompson, mandolin/bass/vocals

Jimmy "Ibby" Ibbotson

When NGDB got hooked up with the greats of traditional country music, I was in way over my head. I was new to the recording studio and what not; they were virtuoso musicians. The band had recorded one LP with me, *Uncle Charlie & His Dog Teddy*. It was well done and covered Jerry Jeff Walker's song "Mr. Bojangles." The album was recorded in Hollywood with the help of two studio drummers (Jim Gordon and Russ Kunkel) and Mike Rubini on piano.

At Nashville cutting the *Circle*, I played a lot of brush drums on a small kit with a snare, hi-hat, and bass drum. Also, I played rhythm guitar on a cut, but it's my harmony vocals that I can hear these days. We (Jeff and Les) sang around one mic with Gary Scruggs, while Maybelle, Martin, Acuff, or Doc Watson sang in all cases. I was a backup singer!

We didn't arrange many of our harmonies that tightly. I can hear my high harmony on the title cut, crossing other vocals like a drunk at a beach party.

I sang the lead on one Hank Williams song, "Lost Highway," strumming my Martin D-41 while I sang. As we cut everything live, there were no overdubs. There was little worry about the guitar bleeding with the vocal, or vice versa. Vassar Clements was playing with Junior Huskey (and us), and they both went out of their way to compliment my approach to the song. They made me feel comfortable, and their playing buoyed my vocal and kept me on pitch. Vassar said, "If I close my eyes, I'd think it was old Hank singing today." Funny thing was, at that time I'd never heard Hank sing it. I had learned it from watching Bob Dylan in his movie *Don't Look Back*.

Jimmy Ibbotson

Bill McEuen asked me to say something before we kicked it off. When I said, "This is going out to all the folks back home" it seemed permanent. My friends and family were back East, and I was living a life with many dangers, tolls, and snares.

There were hundreds of twenty-two-year-olds breaking into the music business who would have been better prepared to record with these legendary singers and musicians. But maybe that is what made the music on *Circle* so special: Fadden was a blues harmonica player, and Jeff and I were singing rock and roll. The guys in our band all had shaggy hair. We didn't share the same political opinions with most of the Nashville cats. And because of the Vietnam War, it was a time when people took strongly opinionated stands. But we were respectful of their age and feelings, and they were happy to be recorded with younger players who were having success on the pop charts.

They (the *Circle* artists) had never been recorded so carefully and cleanly, using such modern processors. We had rarely recorded without the aid of multiple overdubs. In most cases we'd cut a scratch vocal—the musicians laid down the instrumental track. Then, the lead singer would replace the tracking vocal. Then we would lay down our harmonies. Each track would add a bit of noise to the mix . . . and a great deal of emotion was removed. (We didn't have that here because it was two-track.)

It turned out that *Circle* was Maybelle's first gold record! She invented the business of recording country songs (1927, in Bristol, Tennessee) and putting them on the radio. We were kids just imitating what the Carter Family had done, and together we struck . . . platinum.

One of our brothers, Bill McEuen, got us a record deal and put together a historic collaboration. And bingo, Bill was a genius and my hero. The record broke down barriers between generations. And, I was living the life of Forrest Gump to have been a small part of it.

—James Arvey Ibbotson—a.k.a. Ibby

1

THE PATH TO THE CIRCLE

We went to Capitol Records in Hollywood (the round building that looks like a stack of records) to audition for "getting a record deal," but, it didn't work. We were turned down . . . the first of several rejections. Seeing all the albums on hallway walls was inspiring, though, and made me—and some of the other guys—more driven to get that deal. Bill kept shopping us around until Liberty Records said yes.

John McEuen, 1966

Early Nitty Gritty Dirt Band preconcert

They liked one song, "Buy for Me the Rain," which was a folk rock type of song written by friends Steve Noonan and Greg Copeland. It was released February 7, 1967, in LA to become a "regional" hit . . . and actually made it to #35 on the national pop chart. My banjo was prominent in it, and I was happy about that, even though it had a mute on it! The banjo was on the radio! The group had been together about eight months, but it seemed like forever.

I remember this as being the Mecca, a folk club in Buena Park in 1966, where I spent many hours watching the Dillards pre-NGDB. It might have been another place, but Bill was there shooting the nascent NGDB as he often did, and here we have Les, Jimmie, and myself running a song. Every show was exciting to us because we were new and glad to be working . . . still are glad!

No electric instruments yet, as we were doing a lot of acoustic jug band and good-time music, mixing it up with some bluegrass (what Les and I are working on) and a few folk tunes. We had no idea where this was going to lead but had a lot of hopes it would be somewhere good. It was.

Jimmie Fadden on tuba and John McEuen on banjo

Young Jimmie Fadden and John McEuen

Hanging out in some dressing room well before the show, Jimmie had to work on a tuba part. He liked "anything low" for a while, which really amused me because he also played harmonica a lot, which was at the other end of the music scale! We used tuba for a couple of songs, but it was just too big to transport along with the other gear just for one song.

I believe the song is "Sister Kate," for which I am playing banjo with a flat pick, in the jug band style that used a different chord every beat or two. The clothes? St. Vincent de Paul or Salvation Army were all we could afford, and they had a plethora of great suits—pinstripes galore!

Ash Grove

In a sense, this is the place it started. Between the Golden Bear in Huntington Beach and the Grove. You could play both these LA-area venues because they were far enough apart to have separate audiences. The photo on the poster was shot at the Troubadour, and I would stick the W. C. Fields poster up to dress up the stage.

Notice the length of the performances! A six-day run followed by two ten-day runs! Our ten days spent sharing that tiny dressing room with Merle was amazing to us all. The times were good, and our music was "good-time music." We were six months old as a band, knew about fifteen songs, and did them a lot!

It was a "private lesson" with one of America's greatest guitarists, from whom Jeff and I would pick up things that would last us a lifetime. Fingerpicking was a mystery, and one of the main sorcerers in that style was the headliner, Merle Travis.

Some nights playing the Ash Grove over the years (we did it several times after Merle's co-bill) some of us would run up to the Troubadour, a place we would also later play, to catch a snippet of whoever was playing there and race back for our second show. About a mile away, it was easy to do between our two shows a night or after the last show. It was an exciting time for all of us.

One good thing about playing the Ash Grove was the food, with a friendly kitchen that would make us sandwiches at night or one we often raided during a daytime rehearsal. It was at one of those rehearsals for the shows with Merle that a young man—but a few years older than us that seemed like twenty years—came in to watch a bit and asked us if we would like to sign a deal with Liberty Records, and he would produce it. I told him, "we've just signed with them. Dallas Smith is producing," and thanked him. "You mind if I listen a while?" he said and was invited to hang out and watch this nascent group of hippies who knew fifteen songs work on some of them. That was the first time I met the man, Leon Russell, who would become a lifelong friend over the years. He had just finished working on "This Diamond Ring" for Gary Lewis (Jerry's son) and the Playboys and was in from Tulsa trying to get more work.

J. Lee White & the HOWLING BLUES
FRED MACDOWELL
NOVEMBER 4,5,6,11,12 & 13

The west coasts finest blues band, featuring the south side Chicago blues
harp and vocals of J. Lee White. On the same bill, the superb Mississippi
Delta Blues sung and played by one of the masters, Fred MacDowell, in a rare
Los Angeles appearance.

AMERICAS TWO GREATEST GUITARISTS

MANCE LIPSCOMB
&
John HAMMOND

in his first west coast appearence

NOVEMBER 18~27

A feast of blues, old and new. Featuring the very greatest of the old-time Negro songster-guitarists,
plus a brilliant, world-famous young interpreter of country & city blues. This program encompasses
the full range of traditional and modern blues, and is a must for everyone.

MERLE TRAVIS
NITTY GRITTY
DIRT BAND

DECEMBER 2~11

A composer of the stature of Guthrie &
Dylan, Merle Travis' songs such as Dark
As A Dungeon and 16 Tons are mainstays
of American Folk and popular music.
Merles guitar style, known as Travis
picking, is perhaps the most influential

and imitated in America. Be sure to
hear the master himself. Also, on the
same bill, the zaniest of the Jug Bands,
is back, bringing the era of W.C. Fields with them. There's no "Prohibition" on

Ash Grove poster

John McEuen and Jimmie Fadden

"Travelin' Mood" with John and Jimmie

"Travelin' Mood" in play here! One of my first mandolin songs was fun to do up front with Fadden. This is around 1969 and was one of four songs we cut with first take on *Uncle Charlie*, something we would hear about from Mr. Acuff a few years later.

I'm wearing one of the shirts from *Paint Your Wagon* that had been used in movie wardrobes since the 1930s. They quit using it after filming *Wagon*; I kept it.

I always wished Jimmie was up front more on the stage because his quirky personality was not visible from the drums. He came up to do "Honky Tonkin'" later on and killed it. Why the sailor suit is about the same question as why the Mountie suit that Les wore for a couple of years. Why? We could afford them. They were cheap.

Nitty Gritty Dirt Band performing "Collegiana" live

"Collegiana"

One of the most difficult songs to learn (maybe because it was in Eb) was "Collegiana" . . . also one of my favorites. Since Les was playing banjo, I headed to the piano (not visible here), and we got through this 1928 Dorothy Fields and Jimmy McHugh song. It is killer and ended up on the album just prior to *Charlie*, titled *Rare Junk.*

Dorothy and Jimmy were great hit songwriters of the 1920s and 1930s. It has been told that one time they were in their New York office, working on—starting—trying to start, but not finding anything to write about, and they needed a new song. One of them said to the other "Let's go look at the Macy's [some say it was Tiffany's] windows! They're up, and tonight's the first night!" They agreed, and this Lennon/McCartney team of their day ran down to 34th Street to see what they could and maybe get some inspiration.

As they stood looking at one of the many windows, about halfway through their viewing, a young, obviously newly married young couple came up and stood behind them, window gazing, too. The young bride said, "Oh, honey . . . look at all the wonderful things they have! It sure would be good to have . . ." She was cut off her partner, with him saying, "Oh, yes, baby . . . I'd love to get some of those sparklin' things for you too, but, baby, I can't give you anything but love." And they walked away.

Dorothy looked at Jimmy . . . Jimmy looked at Dorothy . . . Jimmie said, "Let's get back to the office!" They scurried back to their songwriting office and "I Can't Give You Anything but Love" was finished that night. They took it to two different Broadway plays, and they both added them to their shows. The rest is history; it became one of the most recorded songs of the century, even Lady Gaga did it (with Tony Bennett).

But "Collegiana"? People did not like it! We worked harder on that song than anything else on *Rare Junk* and eventually dropped it from the set, even though it had what Jeff (the singer) called the "singing flowers," as the background part was called.

The Ice House

The first place I played and made money! But it was with Michael (Martin) Murphey, six months before NGDB came into my life. I knew from performing with the Texas Twosome (as 'the act" was called) and because there were four of us, and me and the other guy (John London, bass) were not from Texas that it was not going to last long for me. But Bob Stane, Ice House manager, paid me, and it felt great!

This was one of the main places for the early NGDB to play and was a nice showroom that held about 240 people. I remember falling asleep on stage when we were there rehearsing for this gig and being awakened by a big train sound, coming right at me! Well, the other band guys, led by Fadden I think, had put all the mics right over my peacefully snoozing self as they went to get burgers. They came back and turned them all on, blasting the PA system with my snoring, and woke me up.

I am not sure we called them "sound checks" yet, but we were there early in the afternoon for the nighttime show, which was sold out. "Buy for Me the Rain" was starting to get airplay on the radio, and the band was starting its 50+-year career.

This PR photo of the NGDB in The Ice House poster was taken in the stairwell of our "Dirt House" on Rodgerton Road in Beachwood Canyon. Those were the days, my friend. Greg and Duane, the Allman Brothers (my brother was going to manage them), would move in to occupy one of the floors of the four-story house with us a few months later, when they came to LA as the Allman Joy, before changing their name to Hourglass.

The Ice House Herald

34 SOUTH BRAND BLVD.   GLENDALE, CALIFORNIA 91204   RETURN REQUESTED   DATED MATERIAL

Held Over

THE TRAVELERS 3
Jan 31 - Feb 5

Releasing their new Tower Hit
"Riot on Sunset Strip"

THE STANDELLS
February 7 - 12

Admission for this Special Show:
Tues—Wed—Thurs: $1.50
Fri—Sat—Sun: $2.00
There will be 3 shows on Sunday,
Feb 12 as Monday is a holiday.

The new sound of the Legendary
Tim Morgon

TIM MORGON
February 14 - 19

With their Capitol hit. . . .
"Rock & Roll Gypsies"

HEARTS & FLOWERS
an 31-Feb 12 and Feb 21-26

NITTY GRITTY DIRT BAND
February 21 - 26

Introducing their new Liberty
single and album.

See him on the
Smothers Brothers Comedy Hour

PAT PAULSEN
February 14 - 19

Ice House concert poster. COURTESY OF BOB STANE, COFFEE GALLERY BACKSTAGE

Playboy After Dark *show*

Playboy After Dark

This photo from Hollywood's Television City the first time there. . . or maybe second. We did Hugh Hefner's *Playboy After Dark* show with the second incarnation of the band, the one that did Paramount Pictures *Paint Your Wagon*. This is one of the last shows we did (December 1968) after *Wagon*. You can tell we did not know quite what to wear, or at least I didn't. It was supposed to be casual. We did "Washington at Valley Forge" (in this photo) and "Alligator Man," songs leftover from the old daze, but Chris Darrow (on the right) killed "Alligator Man" real good!

Somehow some of this bag of mixed nuts was able to continue after we broke up, which was right after this December taping, as the front row here (Les, Jeff, Fadden, and me) is what regrouped six months later, with Jim Ibbotson.

Doing a show like this was fun, took a long time (usually about seven to eight hours), was at "the top of showbiz" game, and worked well with the press. But one wonders if it really mattered. . . . Did it do any good? One of the best things about it was it was taped right next to the Farmers Market, an LA landmark place with dozens of food booths . . . one of the first "food courts."

John McEuen

Hittin' da Note!

Some place lost in time, the Aspen Inn, right after the *Circle*. I was trying to play myself "out of a corner," and not quite making it. I am glad Bill caught this without sound because my Florentine banjo does not look like it is treating me well. That banjo was made in 1927 and should have known the notes by now! But if the song was "Foggy Mountain Breakdown," I did.

I never did wash or clean that leather suit in the two years that I wore it. It is now in the Cleveland Rock and Roll Hall of Fame, standing up by itself next to the replacement banjo I used on *Circle*.

Our agent, Lance, booked the Earl Scruggs Revue with Josh Graves and Vassar Clements (and Gary and Randy) in the same club two or three times. The first booking in Aspen was the same year we recorded *Circle*, that December after. The first Tulagi (club in Boulder) booking, though, Lance did not do and that was when I asked Earl "the question" if he would record with us.

This was a big deal to all of us, getting Earl in our state, and after *Circle* sometimes playing or singing with him. I was living in Idaho Springs the first time they came to play Tulagi and talked Gary in to bringing Randy up to visit. It was about a forty-minute drive, and I gave him instructions on coming up Highway 6 through Golden. After a few hours went by and they didn't show, the phone rang. It was Gary, telling me the canyon they were driving up was too deep and narrow, the mountains too steep and high; they got scared and turned around, and went back to their hotel! We were all kids then. We got together at Tulagi that night and went out to eat after their show. . . . great fun.

Jimmie and Ibby

A rare occurrence, when Ibby and Fadden would sing together on stage. It was 1974, probably the Boarding House in San Francisco, and things were good. We were feeling the effects of a few chart hits and the *Circle* album at this time.

Jimmie Fadden and Jimmy Ibbotson

Uncle Charlie *album cover designed by Dean Torrence*

Uncle Charlie & His Dog Teddy

This cover was a masterpiece in itself. Bill took all the elements and mounted them on a metal plate, let the paint start peeling, and all the elements came together as a cover!

It is worthy of mention that six of the cuts were first takes with no overdubs! We would hear the value of that a year later, but it worked well for us. They were "Livin' Without You," "Travelin' Mood," "Clinch Mountain Backstep," "Randy Lynn Rag," "Billy in the Low Ground," "Swanee River," and one I was especially proud of, "Opus 36."

But there was one that we did seventeen takes on and then started over. I remember it being the last take that we replaced every part to "make it better, tighter, cleaner" but found out that it didn't work! So, we started a new version, and by then, we really knew the song—it was "Prodigal's Return," one of four of the Kenny Loggins songs on this wonderful album. We were still learning to be a band, and it was difficult! But we learned—on-the-job training.

The album would lead us to the ears of Earl Scruggs and open the door for the making of the *Circle* album. It sometimes seems as if it was meant to be, but there were a lot of things that came in to play for *Circle* to happen.

Nitty Gritty Dirt Band live at Lake Tahoe

"Getting Them Going" at Sahara Tahoe

With chart success on *Charlie*, NGDB played Sahara Tahoe around the time of the *Circle* album, not knowing the impact it would have. NGDB's bluegrass always went over well, and we gave them light doses of it . . . just enough. This is the band the Scruggs family would see at Vanderbilt University, with full dress of more costumes that each guy felt appropriate in at the time. The Cajun flavored "Diggy Lo," the song being done here with NGDB flavor was a crowd-pleaser that always "got them going." Ibby's accordion and my fiddle made a nice sound that sounded like a reflection of real Cajun music (at least to us). We must have played this song to as many as Doug Kershaw, who we learned it from in the early 1970s.

My takedown of the words from the record of Kershaw's was phonetic, and I admit to it not being English or French Acadian or anything that sounded like "understandable," and Ibby tore into it like he wrote it. The world of the Juniper Lounge did not know what to think of these hippies who played Cajun, bluegrass, Chuck Berry, Buddy Holly, and some of their own songs to a crowd that spent a lot of time clapping, cheering, and having a great time. Two sets a night at this venue, and we were ready for it. The pit bosses would often complain about the volume, but the band played on, and the curtains of the gambling floor were closed again and again.

Nitty Gritty Dirt Band live at Lake Tahoe

"Stars and Stripes"

Born a few years earlier out of frustration of a show not going over in mid-California, Jeff said, at the end of a set not liked by the crowd, "Well, here's one you will like . . ." and went on to talk about Frankie and Dolores a bit, bumper bullets, and a few things mocking the musical tastes of the 1950s, and we did "Good Night My Love." Much to our astonishment it went over like we were the Beatles and it was their first time in America.

When we got to LA the next week, Jeff had worked up a comedy routine (this is all on the NGDB's *Stars and Stripes* album) that tore the audience up in a different way. It was cool. I did a solo piece while they went backstage to do a costume change, and then Jeff came out solo for about eight minutes of hilarious comedy stuff about the 1950s.

The band would drift out toward the end of his routine, with introductions of each (identifying their "character"), saving the lead singer for "and now here he is . . . ," and Ibby would kill "Good Night My Love" as if a lounge singer. I thought this was a great piece, and it stayed with us through the Vanderbilt show. Jeff decided to drop it as Sha Na Na was coming on then, and it seemed like we might be doing Sha Na Na tribute or such. It was a good choice, as we were using it at the end of a show to make sure we would get an encore. The songs had also gotten better, and the NGDB was getting to a point it could stand on its own legs and take people with us and our music.

I missed doing this, as I loved "show business," but at least my solo spot stayed in the set usually. Those decisions, of what a set would be, were usually by group consensus, but often Jeff would call a few songs or sometimes one of the other guys—but usually Jeff—and it was music we all were doing, so it didn't matter to me; but I missed the costume change! Fortunate that Bill was there all week, he captured this one fleeting moment of lesser-known NGDB history,

"Alligator Man"

One more shot of Bill's in Lake Tahoe, doing the song "Alligator Man" from Jimmy C. Newman. This song killed, but we never recorded it. It was a leftover from the previous NGDB and stayed in for a few months around *Uncle Charlie* time.

Nitty Gritty Dirt Band

Nitty Gritty Dirt Band. L–R: John McEuen, Jimmy Ibbotson, Jimmie Fadden, Les Thompson, Jeff Hanna

While performing at Sahara Tahoe we took a day off (which really wasn't a day off) and spent that day shooting PR photos. This one, taken not far from Lake Tahoe, was shot early in the morning and we were in the middle of the desert. Photos from that shoot, and the one with the train, became the album art for *All the Good Times*.

Doug Dillard, John McEuen, and Ramblin' Jack Elliot

Doug Dillard and Ramblin' Jack Elliot

A great time was had by all! My banjo mentor, Douglas Flint Dillard, sitting in with us a couple of years after release of the *Circle* album—a definite high point in my life at that time. Also, the great "lost wanderer" Ramblin' Jack Elliot on guitar to my left as we jammed on some tune that made that famous Dillard smile flare up, but then again, many things did that!

I was into the Dillards before Earl Scruggs by a year or so. A few other banjo pickers of the time— Pete Seeger, Bill Keith, Don Reno, Eddie Adcock, Billy Faier, J. D. Crowe, and Sonny Osborne— showed up over the next year; all were big influences, too, and always amazing this young banjoist with their tone and notes.

Bill shot this in 1974 at the Boarding House in San Francisco during a NGDB performance, videotaping there that has, to this date, not been seen.

It was a monumental show, with David Bromberg, Commander Cody, Steve Martin (emcee and performing), Linda Ronstadt, John Hartford, Moondog and Mule Deer, and a few others. Bill financed this three-camera television shoot and recoded it in multitrack, calling it *The Lost Television Show*. The recording is of an era that is gone, was dust in the wind, and is fondly remembered by some of us. Linda was great, as were all the others.

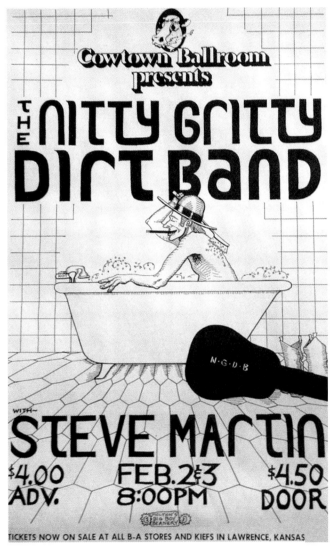

Cowtown Ballroom poster

Steve Martin and Cowtown Ballroom

That year, 1973, was strange in many ways. Word of the *Circle* album was out there, and it was selling; *Uncle Charlie* was still freshly hot and selling; and the band was on the road about two hundred days a year. Tiring. Exhausting. Mind numbing. But it was always with excitement that we would go to perform at Cowtown, the short name for this defunct roller rink that had been turned into a "concert hall," the Cowtown Ballroom. You could still hear the wheels! A crazy crowd of about 2,400 would be crammed into Kansas City's new premier place that was supposed to hold 1,800. Cowtown operated quite heavily between 1971 and 1974. We would go a day early when possible; promotion was fun, and there it was a good time to rest. I was road managing then, too, and that took an extra four hours a day to handle those details. We went to Kansas City often on a much-needed day off, on the way to some other gig, just to hang out. "Everyone" played there, from Arlo Guthrie to Frank Zappa. Check it out on Google, and you will find quite a history.

NGDB was the last act to play, in fact. A sad night it was. As the promoter, Stan Plesser, and I were walking out after that last show, I said, pointing at a sign on the wall, "I don't think anyone will miss that . . . can I take it?" His "yes" led to me taking down the "Parents with Children will need a fee ticket" sign. A treasure from the days gone by. Steve Martin opened for this crazy crowd and did himself good. It was tough for him, but they were easy for us.

Vassar on "Walkin' Shoes"

A couple of years after the *Circle* album, we had Vassar pick with us as often as possible. We had him play on more than bluegrass tunes, but he especially shined when we got to some of the older time songs. Here we are doing "Walkin' Shoes" from the album, a shot that ended up being on the cover of *Stars and Stripes* album of that year. Vassar was always appreciative and played hot . . . with his eyes shut most of the time.

Doing "Walkin' Shoes" a year after *Circle* brought Vassar into some of the NGDB bluegrass live performances. It was great to take a piece of history on the road with us and park those magic notes of his in the ears of the college audience. This was the time period when we asked if he wanted to

L–R: John McEuen, Jimmy Ibbotson, Jimmie Fadden, Jeff Hanna, Vassar Clements

tour Japan with us, and he said "Dad bime! . . . sounds like a good idea! Let's go. . . ," and we did. For a month in this period, right after recording the *Stars and Stripes* album, we took Vassar with us to amaze the Japanese audience . . . and make us sound better! We played about twenty-two shows and performed in a bunch of great halls (about eighteen) averaging 2,200–2,800 seats.

The *Circle* album had started doing quite well in Japan before we got there, and it worked great having him with us.

David Bromberg

David Bromberg did not realize how much we admired him, both as a musician and performer. After the *Circle* album, which came about with a lot of credit given to the *Uncle Charlie* album, we crossed paths with this favorite side musician of Jerry Jeff's many times on the path of his own career. This was during our bluegrass music at the Boarding House, and he sat in quite ably on Dobro, one of the many instruments he played.

It was 1969 when we first met, as "Mr. Bojangles" was just about to be released. I took the band to the Philadelphia club the Main Point, so we could see the writer of the song, Jerry Jeff Walker, meet him, and tell him we were going to release a single of his song. David was also playing with Jerry Jeff as his sideman on this evening.

L–R: Jimmie Fadden, Jeff Hanna, John McEuen, Jimmy Ibbotson, David Bromberg

Uncle Charlie *Hollywood billboard* PHOTO BY JOHN McEUEN

The *Charlie* Billboard!

A crowning achievement! A billboard on Sunset Boulevard in 1969, right in the middle of the music business district. In those days, billboards meant that the group was hot or the label believed in them enough to hype them with one, or that their manager was so good that he could get blood out of their turnip. Whatever the reason (this one was because of our manager), we got a billboard that stayed up for five months!

With Bill's name as album producer visible, I thought it was great that he should get credit. We did not have a hit from *Charlie* yet, so this was a shock to the music businesspeople who had turned us down in the earlier years. "Some of Shelly's Blues," "House at Pooh Corner," and "Mr. Bojangles" were to come from this record—the hits that led to the *Circle* album.

Sometimes, late at night, it was fun to drive by the billboard, about five minutes from my Laurel Canyon place, just to look at it, on the way to see who was at the Troubadour. It was the next year we would move to Colorado, where a lot of unknown was waiting, *Circle*, for one.

2

THE *CIRCLE* SESSIONS

Tut Taylor's Axe

Three people did not make it to the recording sessions. We had asked Bill Monroe (well, we got the question to him) if he would want to participate, but he turned it down. Monroe was focused on his music at the time and did not care about what was on the radio or making the pop charts currently. I believe he thought we used drums, electric guitars, and horns in the music we were doing and would do that with him. I don't blame him. Those who did make it to the album seemed appropriate. He did come up to me several years later at a festival, where I was opening for him solo, and said, "Hey, John if you ever decide to do another one of them *Circle* albums well, give me a call." It was not the time for that then.

Josh Graves, the Dobro player who set the mark for that instrument with Flatt & Scruggs for so many years (1950s), was in my sights as the perfect guy to hold down the Dobro slot, as Oswald Kirby might not be able to do all of it on the album. A month before the sessions I had nervously called Josh, a star to me, and introduced myself, telling him "my plan." He was excited. To have him pickin' with Earl and the others would have been a treat for both he and us, as he brought life to that instrument that made you laugh and did so generously.

I was excited a week later when he called but not with the desired outcome. He told me, sadly "Oh, John, Flatt doesn't want me pickin' with Earl while I'm on his payroll [he was playing with Earl's ex-partner, Lester Flatt, then]. I appreciate the call and the offer, but I'll have to turn it down."

Bill thought he could solve that by getting Tut Taylor in on the sessions. The only other Tut I had heard of before was a king in Egypt. We had known of Tut from an album he made on the West Coast, and he seemed pretty hot. Tut came in, and Earl was there, too (we were kind of "auditioning" him). He played around with his Dobro, and finally Earl ran a song with him. Tut got flustered. He choked. He was sweating. He was uncomfortable. He was under pressure, for sure, but I thought a good pressure.

Earl Scruggs and Tut Taylor

Tut Taylor's Dobro

Nevertheless, after stopping in the middle of "Fireball Mail," he said "I'm struttin' in high cotton here. I don't think I can do this, boys!" He packed up and fled the studio but not before Bill got a shot of his flat-pickin' style of Dobro playing.

Someone—not sure who, probably Earl or Louise—suggested a call to Norman Blake, who was known in the bluegrass world but not a name to us as a Dobro player. Blake had played with Bob Dylan and Johnny Cash, and his overall "credentials" were perfect. He grew up in Alabama and started playing guitar when he was eleven, dropping out of school when he was sixteen to make money playing music. Bill called Norman, who was just two years older than he was, and asked him to play. He came and did all the right notes for us, carving out some history with that bar.

Tut Bows Out, Brother Oswald Enters the Circle

Up close you could see that although Tut used a flat pick, his instrument sounded great. He got a lot of licks out there on recordings we had heard, but was not confident about his playing enough to do the sessions, so he bowed out. He did help Oswald Kirby with the publishing on his tunes, as Oswald did not know nor understand publishing. Then, again, neither did I.

When I was doing the session reports for the AFM union, I was shocked to discover Oswald signed his name with an "X" mark! It did not make me think any less of "Bashful Brother Oswald," but I had never met anyone who did not know how to read and write. He didn't need to because he played with the soul and feeling needed on the songs.

With the music of Hawaii, played by Sol Ho'opi'i and other performers, gaining in popularity, Kirby bought his first resonator guitar, an early National Guitars model (metal guitar with a resonator cone in the middle) and joined in the trend, playing in bars, cafés, and beer gardens. He visited the Chicago World's Fair in 1933, playing in clubs and gaining a following. Some of the clubs he played in were owned by Al Capone.

In a bid to find more steady work, Kirby moved to Knoxville, Tennessee, in 1934. Taking the stage name Pete Kirby, he played resonator guitar with local bands, among them Roy Acuff's Crazy Tennesseans. Pete Oswald Kirby was born in 1911, and by 1939, he was playing with Roy Acuff! As part of the Acuff band, now called The Smoky Mountain Boys, he became a member of the Grand Ole Opry.

My mother said, when she heard the *Circle* album, "who is that man playing the Dobro on 'Sailing on to Hawaii?' I don't know why, but every time he plays that thing, it makes me cry!" I had thought it was because she liked Hawaii, or Oswald, or something. At that point, I realized Oswald made a lot of folks cry with his soulful backup.

And he knew all the words to "Spinning Wheel"—even the naughty ones. He sang it for me (both versions) in Roy's dressing room one night at the Opry, eighteen years after *Circle.* I called my mother that night, from the dressing room, and had him sing "the nice words" to her. That was a big night for me. I put that song instrumentally on my *String Wizards* record in honor of that moment.

Meeting Merle

In those Ash Grove days of 1966, when these Nitty Gritty puppies were first learning how to bark, we were playing a *lot* of ragtime and good-time music, jug band music, and some bluegrass. We had about twenty songs we knew as a band. That is when we met Merle Travis, a major picker and songwriter, especially known then, shown by the full-house crowds he drew for ten days. We opened for him and chatted it up between sets as much as teenagers could do with him. He played music so beautiful it made what we did sound like rinky-dinky music. But we had fun and so did he.

Merle Travis

Merle had written some of the most iconic songs of country music: "Sixteen Tons" (a huge hit for Tennessee Ernie Ford), "I Am a Pilgrim," "Smoke, Smoke, Smoke That Cigarette!" (a huge country standard), and I was just trying to figure out his masterful hot showpiece "Walkin' the Strings." "The Sheik of Araby" is another of my favorites and that we were going to get some of these tunes recorded by him, with us, on our album would be a wonderful thing. Bill made that call to Capitol Records and set it up.

Here you see an example of one of the reasons the album sounds so good: a lot of space between voices, mics, and instrument, making it have more of the "acoustic" of the acoustic guitar. As Merle, born and raised in Kentucky, goes through his coal miner song "Dark as a Dungeon" in this shot, you can see how at ease he is with his music.

Merle Travis

We all knew how important this was, this moment, even though it was only the first day. Merle was singing about the difficulties of coal mining and how tough it is for those miners. We weren't listening to some college "folk singer" in Southern California in a madras shirt doing this song with a nylon string guitar. We were listening to the source. He makes you feel like he knows what he is singing about and that he knows people and what they were going through in the songs. He was from Muhlenberg County, and Mr. Peabody's coal train had not hauled it away—yet.

Fadden and Les do a great job of understatement on this. The harp is barely there, only for support, and the mandolin is mainly for the turnarounds, as if listening and then responding.

Merle Was Ready!

Merle was the first one up, and he was ready. When the band went to his house the previous week to rehearse a bit, it did not seem like it would be this easy. His wife answered the door, saying "Merle, the Nitty Gritty boys are here!" She "confided" in us that he had not played that much and might be a little out of practice. Merle said he would get his guitar out of the closet.

He procured a dusty guitar case and took out a fine instrument, which he proceeded to tune. Travis talked about working on a TV show and not having a lot of time to pick in the past few months . . . and kept tuning.

He hollered to his wife that he could not tell what string was out of tune and could she help. She hollered back it was the B string that wasn't right. He tuned up, saying, "I want to put 'Cannonball Rag' on this album; you know, the one that goes like this . . ."

Merle then proceeded to stumble through a bit of "Cannonball Rag," making it look like he barely knew it. I was thinking maybe we should have gotten here a couple of years ago, but he had a plan, a trap, laid for us, and we fell right in! Merle grinned, and looked at us a second, and proceeded to rip into "Cannonball Rag," and he played it perfect . . . just like he was going to do on the album. He was ready. After we rehearsed, we were ready.

Merle Travis

"Nine Pound Hammer"

When "Nine Pound Hammer" came up, we were all excited because it was an all skate (everyone played or sang). Jeff had the vocals together with Les, Ibby on snare brushes, Fadden on perfect harp, and I played the 5-string.

We got quiet, and Merle started the song, with Fadden coming in just backing up the vocal on the second verse and then perfectly backing up my banjo solo. I had not heard him play so "restrained" in a while! The group worked great together on this, and we did it in one take, too! Putting us a couple hours ahead of schedule. Well, we now had four songs to listen to, so we started with the first one . . . and played them all! And played them all again!

It was such a joyous ending to this, I don't know if it was because we all made it through, everyone was happy, we ended at the same time, or what . . . other than it was just so much fun and we were having it! I did not miss loud amps and monitors that day—not sure I have ever missed them.

Merle Travis

Merle Lays Back

Just before recording Merle, Bill went out to check the mic placement, taking his camera with him. Travis was quietly picking, getting ready to record "Cannonball Rag" with Junior on bass, one of his showpiece tunes that set the mark for a new way to play.

Merle's Picking and Singing

Merle Travis was a mild-mannered guy who calmly walked around without any airs. He knew he played a unique style, but it did not seem to go to his head and let it out with a smile. He would record one of his great tunes, and at the end of it say, "how'd it do? Did we get it?" to which Bill's answer was always "Yes, you got it!"

Travis knocked his stuff out so fast we sat around and I ordered our lunches, and we chilled a bit. We knew we were under way.

Merle Travis

That someone could paint a whole world of life in songs and then play them was Merle for sure. His "Dark as a Dungeon" spoke well of the coal miner like you were listening at the coal mine shaft entrance. "I Am a Pilgrim," you believed what he sang, thinking of him as a pilgrim in the song and then you realize he is.

The genius of music he put into his instrumentals is what drew me to Travis initially. Bill would play "Saturday Night Shuffle" almost every day, as well as a few other Travis tunes. I was enamored with his "Sheik of Araby" and "Cannonball Rag." Jeff was particularly intrigued and in awe at the same time by how Travis backed up his vocal while playing. It was like two people at once!

"Dark as a Dungeon"

Merle Travis had not seemed to age since the NGDB opened for him for ten days at Hollywood's Ash Grove (now the Improv) five years earlier in 1966. Maybe we had aged a bit, as since seeing him in those early days the band had broken up twice, recorded four albums, played in two movies, lost three members and gained one, and here we were with him again. All of us, especially Jeff and I, were enthralled by his playing and calm demeanor.

Travis found greater exposure after an appearance in the successful 1953 movie *From Here to Eternity*, singing and playing "Re-enlistment Blues." The success of Tennessee Ernie Ford's million-selling rendition of "Sixteen Tons" in 1955, which Travis wrote, saw his reputation grow even more.

Merle Travis is now acknowledged as one of the most influential American guitarists and writers of the twentieth century. His unique guitar style inspired many guitarists who followed, most notably Chet Atkins, who first heard Travis's radio broadcasts on Cincinnati's WLW *Boone County Jamboree* in 1939 while living with his father in rural Georgia.

Although his early tutors were among the first to use the thumb pick in guitar playing, freeing the fingers to pick melody, Travis's style, according to Chet Atkins, went on in musical directions "never dreamed about" by his predecessors. His trademark mature style incorporated elements from ragtime, blues, boogie, jazz, and western swing and was marked by rich chord progressions, harmonics, slides and bends, and rapid changes of key. He could shift quickly from fingerpicking to flat picking in the midst of a number by gripping his thumb pick like a flat pick. In his hands, the guitar resembled a full band. Equally at home on acoustic and electric guitar, Travis was one of the first to exploit the full range of techniques and sonorities available on the electric guitar.

Though later, Atkins was the most prominent guitarist to be inspired by Travis, the two players' styles were significantly different. As Atkins explained, "While I play alternate bass strings, which sounds more like a stride piano style, Merle plays two bass strings simultaneously, on the one and three beats, producing a more exciting solo rhythm, in my opinion. It was somewhat reminiscent of the great old black players."

Merle Travis

Travis Style

I have had a few things in my life that seemed like they were meant to be. Some life-threatening, where I dodged the bullet of the end of life; some where I was just at the right place at the right time. Opening for Travis at the Ash Grove in 1966 was meant to be for us, I believe.

This was right place at right time, along with the right instruments and attitude. We were a bunch of young guys playing around "town" (everyone called Hollywood "town"), trying to make a name for ourselves. It wasn't the money, as we were only getting—for the band—about one hundred dollars a night, but club owner Ed Pearl thought we had a future. It was meant to be!

This chord Travis is playing here he used in "Cannonball Rag" (the second chord, after E7), one I could never figure out listening to the record, but we could see it when we opened for him, and Bill thought to catch it in action at the sessions. We called those "the magic chords" because what they created when held and picked seemed to be . . . magic!

Playing at the Ash Grove for ten days in 1967 with Travis was something I will never forget. He was hot, and the notes flew off his guitar. Now, we were in the studio with someone who had a style of music named for him, as "Travis style" was known by every guitar picker for what it sounded like, even though few could do it as well as Travis.

Merle Travis

Merle Travis

Bill had scheduled him first, recording multitrack (sixteen-track MCI), as well as recording at the same time on a Studer two-track). After the first song was laid down in one take, it was obvious the multitrack was not needed and was wheeled out of the studio. The album was going to be recorded in two-track! This would make for greater quality in sound because we were now going to record direct to a master—live. This decision would also save thousands of dollars on tape and postproduction because there would be no mixing!

Travis was scheduled for about four to five hours, but his songs went down so fast it only took about two to three hours. It was a great start. Mostly first takes helped too; he didn't need to rehearse, but others did. He knew what he was doing with that thumb and index finger, which is how he played all his music. I have to use thumb and two fingers to come close to what he did with his two-finger method!

The ever-present cigarette on the peghead, stuck in the end of a string, was good until the end of the song, and kind of a "reward" when he got there. Maybe that is why he wrote "Smoke, Smoke, Smoke that Cigarette!" one of his songs that became a standard for western swing bands like Asleep at the Wheel.

Merle's Secret Chord

Most guitar pickers will say when they want to learn someone's song, that they got most of it, but "there is this one chord . . . I can't tell how to make it." That's what Bill would call "the secret chord," the one you had to figure out. This is one that when you make it, you play the open strings next to what you are fretting, and you will get "an unusual sound," one hard to figure out from a record! Merle had a lot of those and would pull one out when needed, making whatever tune he was playing sound a bit different than you would expect.

You could tell he knew what he was doing as he played, appearing to be relaxed, confident, and sure. But other performers around Merle commented on how insecure he was, how he would talk about stage fright, the crowd, the mic, and the noise but then were amazed at what it was like when he got out there to perform, because it was totally opposite of how he sounded.

Travis-Style Hands

Travis chunked his bass notes, hitting two at a time and making it sound big, as his finger picked the melody. Chet Atkins played more alternating low-end notes and admired the way Travis did so much with his finger and thumb. Merle would sometimes play flat pick licks, holding his thumb pick with the fingers and wielding it like a flat pick. Here he is playing "Cannonball Rag," doing the E7 chord that is in the front of the tune and allowing open strings to ring.

Merle Travis

Smoke, Smoke, Smoke . . .

Don't see this so much anymore, but it did seem to fit him. Sticking the cigarette on the string end was a thing to do back in the day. Bill wanted to catch Travis relaxing between takes, which is what he is doing in this shot.

With his style as well-known as he is, "Travis Picking" is a syncopated style of guitar fingerpicking rooted in ragtime music in which alternating chords and bass notes are plucked by the thumb while melodies are simultaneously plucked by the index finger.

At the age of eighteen, he went out to the world to try his guitar out on "the people." Merle played "Tiger Rag" on a local radio amateur show in Evansville, Indiana, leading to offers of work with local bands. In 1937 Travis was hired by fiddler Clayton McMichen as guitarist in his Georgia Wildcats. He later joined the Drifting Pioneers, a Chicago-area gospel quartet that moved to WLW radio in Cincinnati, the major country music station north of Nashville. Travis's style amazed everyone at WLW, and he became a popular member of their barn dance radio show the *Boone County Jamboree* when it began in 1938. He also performed on various weekday programs.

Humble about it he was, as his upbringing might be said to be a part of that mix. He was inducted into the Nashville Songwriters Hall of Fame in 1970 and elected to the Country Music Hall of Fame in 1977.

Merle and guitar with cigarette

"Cannonball Rag"

Merle relaxing or warming up to nail down the first song, "Cannonball Rag." He knew this recording would be around a long time, I believe, and treated the session as his. It was his, with Junior, and they cooked. Bill used to say to NGDB before a show "Remember what the baker said: 'cook!'" Travis cooked.

"Cannonball Rag" was short enough that his cigarette was only half gone when he finished the song. Then we listened back while he finished it. Imagine, we were set up to record Travis for four or five hours, and this was the first song. They got it in one take, and after listening back a couple of times, we went out to start the next song, "I Am a Pilgrim."

That was about five minutes later, the starting of the next song, from the end of the first one, and listening twice. Travis set the mark for us, and we pretty much stuck to it. We hung on! Ten minutes after the session started, we were getting the second song ready. Ten minutes after that it would be finished.

The second engineer wheeled the sixteen-track machine out of the studio during this pause. It had been running on "Cannonball" also (the first song to be recorded on *Circle*), and we weren't going to need it. Bill decided it was important to stay with the two-track and make it—and us—toe the line even more. No room for overdubs or fixes now! And it would sound a generation better. (The final mix tape would not be transferred from a multitrack, saving making a "copy.") We were making the master as we recorded.

The next song was one take, too! Less than half an hour and two songs were done. The music would be a mixture of songs the artist would pick, or sometimes a request by Bill or me as to a particular song, like "The Grand Ole Opry" that Jimmy Martin sang. Some songs the NGDB intended to do; some came up in the studio (like seventeen-year-old Randy Scruggs playing "Both Sides Now," which ended up sequenced as last) and Oswald Kirby doing "Sailin' on to Hawaii."

Bill always had a love of the islands, and the Dobro started out as Hawaiian guitar in the 1900s with a regular guitar, when a railroad spike was used on the strings instead of fretting them. Then, in the 1930s, the Slovakian Dopyera brothers invented a "resonator" guitar, and called it a Do(pyera)Bro(thers)—Dobro! This made it possible to hear the guitar (it was played regular then) in an eighteen-piece jazz or dance band ensemble. Then the guitar amp was invented.

"Soldier's Joy"

"Soldier's Joy," from Civil War times, is a captivating melody from more than 150 years ago. Back in August, Earl had shown me how he played it—on an open back banjo that had belonged to Uncle Dave Macon. Once I heard it, I knew I had to play that banjo on the song! Earl had bought it from his son Gary, who had bought it from Doris Macon after Uncle Dave had passed. Earl told me he paid a dollar for it, probably worth much more now, but his son Gary told me he thought it was more than a dollar.

Years later at his house, he dug out the "Reuben" banjo from that closet of mysteries for me and let me look at it awhile. This was the instrument he started with at eight years old playing "Reuben's Train" in three-finger style, to be known as "Scruggs picking" as time went on. I held it for a while—maybe five minutes—musing with him about all the changes in music that simple little instrument had created and what he did with it led to. I don't think he had an idea of how far his fingers would reach.

I asked him to take it back . . .

John McEuen and Earl Scruggs

John McEuen and Earl Scruggs

Another Angle on Earl and John's "Soldiers Joy"

The camera caught us over Dino's shoulder, with the VU meters between us, as they set up for and we were running "Soldier's Joy." A few minutes later, Bill went out to the studio and got that other angle, the one I cherish to this day. When I look at these shots now, they make me feel like I am twenty five again. I can still hear the music and feel the sounds. We should have recorded more, but we were there for a driven purpose, and we had a lot of things to get done. I still had to learn "Lonesome Fiddle Blues," which I had heard for the first time a couple of days prior. Junior is working on his bass part, finding some "special" notes to add to the sparse arrangement.

Earl was great to work with. Very patient, and "allowed" you to make mistakes. But when he did "Flint Hill Special" (which he did seven times to get the "right" one), the "group" was not gelling enough for his ears. It was perfect with Flatt, but here? "Let's do one more" he said five times and once by Bill. We agreed the seventh one was hot enough. It was and still is. The band was tight and stayed together. Earl not only played it perfect, he also got the difficult ending perfect each time! Vassar managed to stay on top of it (the seventh take) like it was first take, too. Ibby's snare was pushing right along . . . all was good!

John and Earl Feel the Joy

I went to a happy space for sure listening back to "Soldier's Joy" with Earl. The reason this album came together was because of him, but this moment was mine to relish. Thanks to the Dirt Band it happened. I knew Earl was there because he said "I'd be proud to" when I asked him if he would record with us, but I knew I could not have asked that question without the group behind me; that's what would make it enticing. He had his plans, too.

This song needed to be done I felt, though only with two banjos and bass, and there it was, captured forever on tape and record. I felt it was important to capture the essence of the blending of the two styles and thought I was the perfect person to do it with Earl. Arrogance? I don't think so. Confidence or assurance? Maybe. It just seemed like the right people and one of them was me. Thank you, Earl and NGDB and Gary Scruggs, and Louise, for making the conditions right so it happened and to brother Bill for producing and capturing this magic photo of the moment. This will always be one of the best moments of my life, one I am extremely proud of, and what I was hoping would happen from first seeing Earl at the Opry on that hot summer night with Bill in August 1964. This was only seven years later.

I was happy with Uncle Dave's banjo Earl had loaned me for "Soldier's Joy" and thinking what a privilege to play it in "kind of" Uncle Dave's style, against Earl's three-finger, complementing each

John McEuen and Earl Scruggs

other perfectly. That old banjo sounded great, even though it had the same strings from Uncle Dave's last performance with it at the Opry in the early 1950s.

Gary told me years later that Earl loved this cut, and that made my day. The arrangement was worked out with Junior the week prior at the rehearsals at the Scruggs house in Madison.

The frailing playing once through, then Earl's three-finger once through, then splitting it half and half with each other, then together once through, and ending it. It worked!

I have about five other cuts of music I have recorded in my life for which I will always be grateful; this is one of the top five.

Capturing the Magic

I have been more amazed in retrospect how Bill did it, capturing these magic moments so well, catching the subjects at a just right moment. He didn't take a lot of pictures, because there was little time with the other producing chores. He had to keep moving. He would pick up his trusty Nikon every now and then, snap a few, then put it down for a while, waiting for the next moment.

Here, Earl and I had just gone through "Nashville Blues," which was only "blue" to me in that it was in a minor key. He liked my backup, never questioned what I played, and accepted me as

John McEuen and Earl Scruggs

equal. I was not equal in my mind, just hanging on, playing in G-minor, tuning at the seventh fret to complement his D-minor tuning, which he played open. For banjo pickers, that is the Reuben tuning, the minor version of it, by lowering the third string half a step.

"Nashville Blues" is a captivating tune and made a good record, but I don't think a lot of bands play it. It is not "flashy" nor does it have tricks or hot note sequences, but it came out beautiful with the NGDB adding its touch. Jeff's washboard adds a frequency that is only occupied by him, coming in on the guitar solo and then laying out on certain sections.

Earl Grooves!

As he listened back to "Flint Hill Special," I wondered if he liked it as much as I did. I remember the first time I heard it, with those tuners "doing the strings" like they did. It seemed to be—well—the only word that really comes to mind is "outrageous." Totally unexpected, clever, inspired, genius,

Earl Scruggs

crazy all at once. Earl invented the tuners, called Scruggs tuners, that did that (later modified by great banjo picker Bill Keith) and knew how to use them.

Over the years, some have taken to using tuners more, but it often seems like the "trick" is the purpose, rather than the tune. The trade-off in "Earl's Breakdown" between guitar and banjo made it seem like a conversation being had, a natural thing, the way they go together.

Earl played the "Flint Hill Special" correctly seven times and was waiting for the band to be a band and play with him. On that seventh time they did it, and all came up to the mark. Of course, I was in pickers' heaven, being able to watch him go through it so many times from the control room. He got one of his most difficult endings every time, too.

Earl Scruggs, Just Banjo

How one man could change the world of music is worthy of study. Earl was simple in his complicated approach, one that had to do with "his touch" on the strings with his right hand, and his left hand would keep up to the lightning notes that flew out of the banjo. Earl did not know (nor need

Earl's Banjo

to know) all the chords and names of notes on the neck, but the notes he would choose were the ones that needed to be found.

Other banjo pickers would look for years to the ways he played, trying to sound like him. How he held his hand with the picks on fingers, the gauges of his strings, placement of his bridge, height of strings on the neck, ("well, they're low when you push them down") type of nut (where the strings go to the tuners), spacing of the strings (tightness of the banjo head, height of bridge), but Earl could pick up any banjo and he would still sound like Earl. It was his right hand that made it happen.

The notes he would leave out, as well as the ones he played, made him distinctive as well as part of his sound. Like Vassar Clements (who did not read music nor chord charts) and Oswald Kirby (who could not read), he knew what notes would sound good before he got to them. I have tried to emulate Earl my whole life, but I fall into the pit of banjo pickers who sound like each other, but not Earl. I was happy with my playing, glad he liked my version of "Randy Lynn Rag" on the *Uncle Charlie* album and yearning at the same time to make a mark of my own. But I wish I could sound like him, too! He does seem older, though.

Here Earl is playing "Nashville Blues" while we worked out our parts in the control room. I should say "I worked out my part" because he knew what he was doing. His only tune I am aware of in D-minor tuning (open chord is D-minor), I am glad it is on this record! Earl, like I said to my Mom, "thanks for having me."

Jeff was to play his washboard, Les, mandolin, and Fadden was out in the studio working on harp lines with Vassar and Randy. Someone was ordering lunch. Bill was shooting photos. Junior was waiting and watching the action. After about twenty minutes, we started the song. It was a long day that happened quick.

"Nashville Blues"

I wish I would have had a better banjo for the *Circle* sessions, but it wouldn't have mattered really. I could have used Earl's banjo, but it still would have sounded like me and not him. Regardless, here I was doing three-finger Scruggs style with the guy who invented it. As far as I knew then (or even now), I was the first banjo picker to record with Mr. Scruggs and that weighed heavy on me—until the music started. He made it flow like water.

John McEuen and Earl Scruggs

"Nashville Blues" is in D-minor, and Earl tuned his banjo to D-minor tuning for it, giving it a unique sound. I put my banjo in G-minor tuning, capoed at the seventh fret, and played a second part to his lead. What a day that was for me, as I got to pick with the icon of banjo pickers. I grabbed my picks and hung on. Glad it was not a "complicated" tune because I love it when you do not have to think about what you are going to play and just let it flow. I was already familiar with G-minor because my tune "Dismal Swamp" was in that key.

Like all of Earl's tunes, each one has a different intro, like this one. Then, the major chord was so unlike what one would expect and fit nicely. Earl does the muting of the strings for backing up the guitar solo (played by Randy Scruggs) and changes the pattern during the fiddle solo. Very clever, and one of the secrets of his playing—never too much. I did it during the Dobro solo (string muting) and then Les took it on mandolin. Earl, just by playing with him, made my banjo sound better!

Jeff's washboard with woodblock and the clickety-clack of that "instrument" made it sound more like Nitty Gritty from a few years previous, and he played perfect in all the right spots. Jimmie on harp, doubling with Vassar, was really hot; Vassar loved playing with him, and Jimmie made us all proud of his young expertise, holding his own with genius Clements. They made a new sound for bluegrass with those parts, and it worked.

"Nashville Blues for Real"

Rehearsing "Nashville Blues" with Earl was one thing, and then going into the studio to cut it was quite another. It was as if I knew all the notes. Even the ones I wasn't going to play came out of nowhere, led by sitting next to Earl. Wearing my vest from *Paint Your Wagon* (hey, it was only three years earlier!) made me feel comfortable, but hitting the notes was even more comforting. Like playing pool with someone better than you, I played fine to Earl's lead, laying out until the part came up in the arrangement, which was only ten minutes old.

Randy Scruggs was lead guitar, and his notes rang true, coming in right after his dad with his lead followed by "the section" of Vassar and Fadden. Norman Blake shined on Dobro as he picked

John McEuen and Earl Scruggs

his way through his solo, leading up to Les doing his fine solo he had worked up for the song. Then we got to play it through two more times before the end! I didn't want it to end.

The chords for this tune were what Earl wanted and could not be played by Flatt. To my knowledge, this was the first recording of this song, and stands as good NGDB bluegrass! Washboard by Jeff rounded out the percussion with Earl's horse clops on the "banjer" keeping time when he thought the instrument should not play notes.

Earl's Lesson

I had sat with the man's iconic recordings for several years, trying to figure out what he was doing. He had been a person I wanted to meet, from my dork-like Orange County teenage perspective, to explore that strange world of bluegrass of which he was a part—one of the original creators—but I didn't have a clue *how* to do that before NGDB came along. Earl was a huge star to me, more than any music or movie star.

Earl liked good singing, and Jeff and Ibby were great at that, sounding like the Everly Brothers or the new "country rock" we were formulating on the West Coast, along with a few others. I was more than excited he came to meet me with the NGDB when we played Vanderbilt that night. When he left that evening, his comment "we should record something together sometime" was tossed out to the room, and appreciated by all. To me it seemed an offhand comment, kind of a compliment, since he had not seen our show yet.

Ibby and Jeff's ideas of half-time drums for a song like "Some of Shelly's Blues," (kind of a basic rock "feel") with frailing banjo kicking it off in 4/4, and the "walk down" bass line of Les's made for an interesting record. Ibby sang it great, and Jeff's harmony was perfect. Jeff's rendition of "Mr. Bojangles" with NGDB (the only electric instrument being Les's bass) was not yet in the Grammy Hall of Fame, but it would be! "Mr. Bojangles" became iconic for yet-to-be-named Americana Music and was perfect for the band; he also played washboard and played it well. It became part of the sound for some of the albums; in anyone else's hands, it might have been too dominating (read "annoying"), but Jeff had a good head for arrangement that he put into songs, whether with vocals, drums, guitar, or washboard.

Jimmie's masterful harmonica (harp) would fit in perfectly with Vassar's fiddle on "Nashville Blues," and they were working on their parts, getting ready, while I worked on two-part with Earl. Fadden's developing ideas on drums were good and getting better; and his sparse NGDB guitar

Earl teaches John some licks

work was always innovative and made me wonder what drew him away from that pursuit. But with the harp, he had studied (through records) the masters: Charlie McCoy and Sonny Terry, two of the best (country and blues harp masters), and was headed to notoriety with an instrument he jokingly called a "toy."

Les and his mandolin were ready for pickin' and he bore down on it like a champ, reminding me of earlier days of us playing bluegrass at McCabe's. He was always serious and paying attention to the music overall but focused on his mandolin, trying to get it as good as possible. If we had only known then what we had been practicing for!

Now, I was picking with Earl, getting ready to do "Nashville Blues" with the Dirt Band in the studio. I was excited about *this* recording because I would (as far as I know) be the first banjo player to record with Earl Scruggs. I had to make it good. (Gary Scruggs told me that he did a recording, not a "record," at a festival with Don Reno, someone he also admired, but as it was a live stage show, he does not know where that went.) I do not take that lightly, nor do I ever want people to think the Dirt Band's banjo player "got a big head" because he was the first to pick with Scruggs. Others came after me. Earl's consistency made it easy because I could always count on him being where he wanted to be musically. I just rode along with him, and the band knew their parts.

Life was good. Earl brought peace to those around him somehow . . . that I still try to understand to this day. I think some of it was through music, but that might have been an "extra," a vehicle, a way to express himself to the world that he was a nice guy. It is hard to be mad at a banjo player.

"Soldier's Joy" on the Banjo

The song "Soldier's Joy" dates back to the Civil War days and is captivating to those who hear it. It is even more transporting to those who are playing it. I had wanted to record this with Earl a few years into my early playing but did not know how to do it, how to get that done; I didn't have a band, and I did not know Earl! NGDB started, we played Vanderbilt University, and when I met Mr. Scruggs, I knew it was possible.

Earl Scruggs and John McEuen

"Soldier's Joy" was a song about morphine, being the one thing that was used extensively during the Civil War to alleviate pain. The song was one take—one quick take. We had rehearsed it at his house a few times with Junior the prior week. While I was a fan of one-take recordings, I wanted to pick some more! But one take in the studio was all it took to get it, and even though I asked if he wanted to do it again, we didn't. Earl's response of "I don't reckon why . . . did I make a mistake on that one?" No, I told him, and my part was fine so, we moved on to the next tune.

Maybe it was because I was using the Uncle Dave Macon banjo? It still had the same strings on it from when Uncle Dave had last played it on the Opry in the early 1950s, I was told. It sounded perfect, and I would not see Uncle Dave's banjo again until Earl loaned it to me to do "Carolina Traveller" and "Cripple Creek" on my *String Wizards* album (Vanguard Records), twenty years later . . . same strings, same bass, too, only this time it was Junior's son, Roy Huskey.

If there is one moment I would like to relive in my professional life, it would have to be this one. Earl and me picking. Whew.

Earl and John kicked back on "Soldier's Joy"

"You are My Flower" Mystery Solved

This was a big deal, to have Earl play guitar with his magic touch on the strings, doing "You Are My Flower," as Jeff and Gary Scruggs sang two-part harmony together. Earl was a huge fan of Maybelle and wanted to play the guitar just like her. He said her playing influenced his banjo, though I am not sure how.

I am on banjo, Blake on Dobro (foreground, back to camera), Randy doing the harmony guitar, Ibby on snare/brushes, and Fadden adding the often-needed (especially when doing Carter Family music) autoharp. Fadden is barely visible, behind Earl. Jeff sings a great lead on this quiet song, showing his understanding of Carter Family songs, one which came from studying the music over the years. The two-part harmony is with Gary Scruggs, who grew up with the Carters in his life.

I would find out years later that the lick that comes on the five chord came from Maybelle and the Carter Family being in El Paso for several months, doing a radio show, and her falling in love with Mexican music—and the food. Here that lick reflects what mariachi horns might have played for a few bars or in a few actual bars. The second time it happens, Randy comes in with a guitar harmony part that makes it sound even more like a horn section, with Blake's Dobro answers.

Earl told me years later, that when they recorded this song on the 1961 Flatt & Scruggs' album *Songs of the Famous Carter Family*, that his guitar part wasn't quite right, according to the "audience," Maybelle Carter. The Foggy Mountain Boys took a break for a bit while recording the song, and she came out to the studio and played the solo through for him with just the bass player. Earl

"You Are My Flower" recording. John McEuen, Norman Blake, Randy Scruggs, Junior Huskey, Earl Scruggs, Gary Scruggs, Jeff Hanna

said he would do it that way when everyone came back to the session. It was unlike bluegrass at the time to do an arrangement that way.

Then their engineer piped in "That's OK. You don't need to. We got it." He had cut the tape with the part Maybelle just played into the version the Foggy Mountain Boys recorded, taking out Earl's solo and replacing it with Maybelle's. This explained something I had wondered about for years! Why did the rest of the band on their record drop out for that solo, leaving just the guitar and bass doing the song for just that section? It was because they weren't there! Maybelle's time was exactly the same as the track Flatt & Scruggs was doing, and it matched up perfect.

That's Gary Scruggs holding the paper with the words on it for the song as they were rehearsing. Bill shot this right at the right time.

Earl and Maybelle

When I bought the album Flatt & Scruggs's *Songs of the Famous Carter Family*, I didn't know anything about the Carter Family. It was an album with Earl Scruggs on it, which drew me to it. The music from that album took me away. At first I didn't realize Earl was playing guitar in Maybelle's style, "The Carter Scratch," I learned it was called, and doing it quite well. Earl often said in later years Maybelle's playing was a big influence on his banjo playing. Melody and syncopation were the main focus of attention, and he played the guitar with the same conviction as banjo, with the same picks as he used on the banjo.

You can hear the magic of his timing, or touch, even on the first couple of notes; they are somewhat muted pickup notes and do much better than just the typical lead-in. The only other person I have heard Earl's "sound" on the guitar (and on banjo, he did the same) was Sonny Osborne of the Osborne Brothers. He idolized Earl, but I didn't know things like that at the time of the sessions. I was still from California.

Earl always concentrated, like Bill captures here in this photo, on what he was doing and would play it right every time. He knew this music well and had high regard for Maybelle's contribution. They were friends and saw each other often.

Asking Earl why they did the *Songs of the Famous Carter Family* album tribute, he responded:

Well . . . Mama Maybelle wasn't workin' in music in the late 1950s/early 1960s. She couldn't get work at the Opry or on the road. She'd taken the only job she could find at the time, working as a nurse in a

Earl Scruggs

Nashville hospital, and did that a few years. I wanted to get her back in front of people and performing, and get her music known so people knew that some of those songs they already knew and we sang came from the Carters. Flatt and I decided to put out this album to get that done . . . and, I think it worked!

It was the idea of his wife Louise, I would later find out, as she was extremely clever in those avenues.

The Flatt & Scruggs album *Songs of the Famous Carter Family* was a main influence on me (and, later the band) and showed us a style that we could not ignore, songs the guys wanted to sing. We knew Carter songs were to be on *Circle*, and any of them was fine with Maybelle, and some of them came from this album. But then, they came from her.

Earl's Flat Top Guitar Secret

Often trying to "decipher" licks on various instruments while in those early McCabe's days, people would argue about how something was played. "I think he did it like this" was said often, and they might play the right notes, but it just didn't sound right. Something to do with a combination of things: flat pick, finger pick, flat pick with fingers, capo, open tuning . . . whatever! We didn't really know. It seemed there was some secret to their playing, one that was simple, yet complicated.

Would he use finger picks or play it with a flat pick? We didn't know for sure until we recorded "You Are My Flower" with him, as you can see here—fingers! Fingers with picks on them were the secret. Actually, the secret was who was playing and it was their style of playing.

Earl, an aficionado of Maybelle's playing, did it right. We got to hear and watch that magic unfold in front of us as we went through this Maybelle song and drew off of his energy. I was particularly fond of Earl's guitar with Flatt & Scruggs and would try to do that style on several NGDB recordings over the years. For me it stemmed from "God Loves His Children" on one of the older Flatt & Scruggs albums, a guitar finger style I tried to reflect on *Will the Circle Be Unbroken, Vol. III* with Vince Gill on "All Prayed Up."

Earl Scruggs

"You Are My Flower"

While Earl's love of Carter Family music is focused on the playing of Maybelle, here we see him up close, doing what has become known as the "Carter scratch," with picks on and in action. Using the U-87 Neuman mic on the guitar, with enough space to pick up the guitar acoustically and yet keeping it somewhat separate from other instruments, was Bill's choice based on previous recording experience. He did not like the isolation booths for everything, blocking acoustic sounds bleeding from other instruments or singers, but instead liked the live feel of open mics, also picking up a little bit of what was around that instrument. This recording exhibits the best of both worlds.

"You Are My Flower" is being picked here, as we went through this song a couple of times before recording to get the balances right. After all, we were recording two-track only at this point, the first day, after Travis.

Playing banjo with Earl, backing him up, was a wonderful time. I had asked him his "theory of backup" playing. It was simple: "When they sing high, play low; when they sing low, play high, and no one can understand two people talking at the same time." And fill in after the words go by at the end of the word usually.

Earl's restraint is best exemplified on "I'm Thinking Tonight of My Blue Eyes," where he plays harmony on banjo to Maybelle's guitar lead and chunks rhythm during the other solos. He used the same approach on "Keep on the Sunny Side." When Earl played guitar on "Wildwood Flower," Maybelle was on autoharp and singing and me on banjo. It was good for me.

Earl's version of the Carter Scratch

Gary Scruggs

Gary Scruggs was one of the nice things that made it run smooth for us during the rehearsals and recordings. A couple of years younger than me (he seems older, though), sarcastic and funny, he was a good singer with his own voice. Gary was also an excellent songwriter, which I would find out about years later when "The Lowlands" came into my life. He had taken one of his father's instrumentals, "Sally Ann," partly as the basis for one of the most haunting songs in country music, "(I'm Headed for) the Lowlands."

Scheming with Louise Scruggs, with whom I had become late-night email friends (later in the 1990s), I arranged over the internet for Jeff's son, Jaime, and my son, Jonathan, to record "Lowlands" with us, for *Circle III*. I went to her house a few weeks prior to get a demo to send Jonathan, telling him my plan—record this with Jaime and us. The NGDB would make a haunting music video from that with the boys, and they would get a record deal from that with MCA—seemed as if the *Circle* would keep going.

Les was staring at Earl in disbelief, as it was not too many years earlier he was in McCabe's hanging out, fifteen years old, with a mandolin. No one dreamed in 1965, before NGDB actually

Jimmie Fadden and the Autoharp

formed, that we would make such an important record and be an important part of it. We didn't even know it then, while we were making it, how important it was going to be. It was something we just had to do, wanted to do; it was there to do, and we did it!

While we were doing it, though, there was no time for thoughts about the people we were working with after the first day. It was still fun to watch them while they worked and think about how fortunate we were. Here Bill got us good; we are rehearsing "You Are My Flower," a good shot of "cool" Jimmie on autoharp, Les, and Jeff eyeing Earl, and Gary Scruggs also singing.

Jimmie Fadden and the Autoharp

Sitting around the coffee table at McCabe's we would pick various songs, and if you knew the chords and could use your fingers, you too could play the autoharp! Fadden liked to play it around that table as it gave him (and us) respite from harmonica for a while. There was a certain style—Maybelle's, actually—that he had to learn, and he became quite adept at it. He picked it up here for "You Are My Flower," and it filled those spaces invisibly but not inaudibly. Fadden and the autoharp are an important part of this song, as he filled in sonically the space left by the openness of the guitar, there was no mandolin, and the banjo was mainly percussive "chinks."

Randy played the harmony to the lick Earl plays between sections of the verses and saves the harmony part for the second time through. Gary and Jeff shared the vocal chores as two-part harmony, with Jeff's solo lead coming finally in the middle for a verse. Norman Blake on Dobro (not visible) handled the fills that were the answers to the guitar and vocals and sounded like Josh Graves, which was just right!

I had heard this first on Flatt & Scruggs's *Songs of the Famous Carter Family* when I was about nineteen, one of my favorite albums of theirs. It exposed me to a lot of Carter Family music, and when Earl told us "Maybelle is 'in' . . . She wants to do it," Bill and I were elated. This was the real thing and doing this song (without her) was a perfect homage to her. We only had a chance to go through this one once for rehearsal and then record that day. But we did do it a few times at Earl's house the week prior where we rehearsed a bunch of the tunes in preparation for the coming week.

Pickin' School with Merle

What a school to go to, where you could learn from someone you knew a few years earlier and now you have him trapped in the studio! And Merle Travis was a master picker. Fingerpicking? Jeff picked up a lot from Travis, augmenting his folk style, and getting pointers on his playing that I still hear today. The good influence that never goes away if you open yourself to it. Since playing with Merle at the Ash Grove early in 1966, Jeff had come a long way. Being around Merle he knew there was a long way to go, but Jeff got more out of the experience than many.

Merle wasn't quite sure of some of what Jeff was doing, as it would go from one version to another, a lick would "show up," or he would improvise on the fly. Well, he was sure with what he was going to do, but not sure what it would be. It reminds me of what Gary Scruggs told me back then about my banjo playing, something like "I love to see you play yourself in to a corner, because what you do to get out of it is better than what you were going to try and do." He was right.

Merle Travis and Jeff Hanna

"Tennessee Stud"

In the pre-NGDB time (at eighteen), I had not heard of Doc yet. Then I first experienced his music and had not heard of Deep Gap, North Carolina, where he made his home. It was the *Newport Folk Festival* album on which he was one of the "traditional" acts playing to the folkies in 1964 where he burned up "Ticklin' the Strings" for the rabid audience. That he could play that fast and still talk while playing blew me away in my second year of guitar playing. This tune, written by Jesse Fuller, was a great one to pick (I recorded it thirty years later with David Grisman Quartet on *String Wizards II*), as I knew it was hot.

Here he is getting ready to "make an old record," "Tennessee Stud," a story song about a young man from that state who—well, listen to the song. It is one of the best on the *Circle* album.

For this song it was especially cool that he said something about Jimmie's harp, which he liked a lot already, before the song. He complimented everyone along the way, like with this song:

Doc: "Do we wanna try a break? Now your fiddle break comes right after I whip her brother and her paw. . . . Now, that's about pretty a bass line I've heard played in a long time. I compliment that boy back there. That's a horse's foot in gravel . . . that ain't a train. (about the harp) runnin' thru a ford in a creek. Let's see if we can put down a take. Where's the harmony? Right here?"

Jeff was standing right next to Doc doing his harmony job perfect, with Fadden's harp as mournful and sparse, as needed. Playing banjo on this song, headphones on and eyes shut, about midsong it felt as if I was listening to an old record, cut in 1938 or such, only I (and the other guys) were on it, too.

Over the years, I sometimes might comment like this was my album, but people do that, I have noticed, in the film business. The grips, sound man, painters, carpenters all say things like "this is the movie I'm making" when they talk about the film they are working on. It was everyone's album, but it was the one I was making at the same time. It was Jimmie's. It was Jeff's. It was Les's. It was Ibby's. It was theirs, for sure, and everyone else's, but then the gold and platinum records on my wall for *Circle* have my name on them. (Of course, they do, I am in my house.)

Fadden's mournful harp was perfect at 2:49. Vassar's fiddle rang true and came in just right. I did the "Earl's string mute trick" for one verse and loved every minute of this tune. Doc went on performing without us, and "Tennessee Stud" became a "most requested song" of his shows, often finding him ending a set with it. It was "his hit" it seems, and he always did a great job on it.

Doc Watson

"Way Downtown"

We knew (in our minds) that young Jimmie Fadden was a "hot" player at the beginning of NGDB. I believe the *Circle* album showcased his harp talents more than most of our other albums and shows him off in good light. After all, we were recording in a room where one of his influences, Charlie McCoy, had blown notes himself, so he had to come up to the mark. Fadden's tone with his harp is most important because he can draw a long note and keep it slow and "fat," making it fill up the track, making it like a string section. There are some who can play faster notes, fiddle tunes, and such, but Fadden's natural soulful playing (as he does with other instruments) stands out.

Playing with Doc drove all of us to perform at "better than best" for us. Jeff singing on this take right next to Doc and sounding like an authentic old-timer was especially cool to me, matching his phrasing exactly—not easy, but showing what a good (quick-study) harmony singer he is.

We first heard "Way Downtown," an old-time standard, at McCabe's Guitar Shop about five years before doing *Circle.* In fact, it was before NGDB had even formed; we were just a bunch of dreamers sitting around the coffee table, picking. Doc had recorded with Clarence Ashley and Clint Howard and now with us. In those McCabe's days, staring at the album as the music played, we could only imagine what it would be like to pick like Doc. Everyone tried "Black Mountain Rag," but few could do it. Well, actually no one could do it like him.

Jeff encourages Doc to "take another one" during Doc's guitar solo. It was so relaxed with Doc that conversations like that were listened to, and he paid attention. We were really glad because the licks that came out on that second pass are on the record, instead of being talked about. Les's cool solo after Vassar was a surprise even to Les! But Doc loved Les's playing and knew he had played "Clinch Mt. Backstep" on the *Uncle Charlie* album. Vassar's gift was being able to play "modern notes," jazz-influenced notes, and fit them right in to whatever the song was, like he did briefly here. I was frailing away on that Uncle Dave banjo, having the time of my life in C-tuning, being in this old-time band. I felt like Clarence Ashley or Clint Howard.

Doc Watson and Jimmie Fadden

Rings Like a Bell!

The guitar that "rings like a bell," as Merle Travis said, is seen here getting ready for "Way Downtown" and all the hot notes Doc could throw his pick at. Jimmie on harp sat right next to Doc, which made them both comfortable because Jimmie was a great player. He and Vassar had not worked out a twin part yet, so he just took it with banjo riding along. Fadden's harp playing was influential and spread around the music world, influencing the playing of Mickey Raphael (plays with Willie Nelson) and Greg "Fingers" Taylor (Jimmy Buffett's harp guy). They both said Jimmie's playing inspired them a lot, and it sounds like it.

"Way Downtown" became a staple of traditional music for years and at bluegrass festivals around the country. It is a parking lot favorite, letting everyone show off "what they can do with it."

Doc flat picked on the *Circle*, but it should be noted that his fingerpicking was exceptional as well. He also played banjo on a few numbers over the years and gave it that true North Carolina approach—and he was from North Carolina!

Doc's guitar

Jeff and Doc

One of the nice things we did on *Circle* was not play sometimes! You don't want three rhythm guitars on "Way Downtown," as Doc covers it all. And Jeff will never play like Doc Watson. But then again, none of us could. We all want to play like Doc. None of us come close!

Jeff was in a dream world, though, singing with Doc Watson—right up close. Teenage Jeff never thought (well, none of us did in those McCabe Guitar Shop daze) he would get to make a record with Doc, and here he was, doing just that with his band. His voice has the ability to match up with many (something some people can do but has to be worked at), a talent I admire from afar, and saw him do that under pressure here. It was cool he was right there next to him.

Jimmie, sitting to the left of Doc, was perfect, as Doc loved the "boy on the harp" a lot. Jimmie had to "come up to the mark," which he did here fine. I thought the banjo solo was where Fadden starts to play, and Doc says, "let's hear that banjo, too!' while we both played at the same time and it worked!

Imagine being able to tell Doc Watson to take another solo! I didn't have the nerve to do that.

L–R: Jeff Hanna, Doc Watson, Jimmie Fadden

Jeff Hanna, Doc Watson, and Jimmie Fadden

Here Fadden, realizing the importance of in-tune harps, checks his with Doc while Doc talks to Jeff, as they get ready to cut "Way Downtown." Made popular or known by people like Gid Tanner and the Skillet Lickers, Doc usually played this song in his sets, as it would lend itself to hot licks both between vocals and the solo; this is the one where Jeff (at his immediate right, his singing position on this tune) said at the end of Doc's solo, "take another one, Doc," which he did! Thanks, Jeff! Doc's second solo was even better than the first, which was great in itself.

History Made: Doc and Merle Meet for the First Time

One of the plans Bill and I had was to capture on tape Doc and Merle meeting for the first time. It was an astounding moment—a historic event. Bill had asked Merle to come by on the day we were to record Doc to meet up with him, just for that purpose. It was the day after Merle's session, and he liked visiting the studio, where he would "pop in" over the next few days. I remember, in position for the next song, Merle strolling in the back door of the studio, back by Junior. As he walked up to Doc and started chatting, introducing himself, Bill was frantically motioning to me from the control room to move Merle closer to the mic or the mic closer to him—something!

I had to "barge in" to the middle of them as they started to chat, fumbled with the big mic stand and excused myself, asking them to wait just a minute "for technical reasons." Then I asked Merle to get him to restate his comments, "Is this the first time you met Doc?" and stepped away, letting them chat. What transpired between these two musical giants were magic moments for us, captured by the always running 3¾ inches per second (ips) tape. I had to reload it every couple of hours. It went like this:

Doc: "I didn't play guitar until the early '60s"

Merle: "The early '60s?"

Doc: "The early '60s.

M: "Dad Gum!! Yeah (answering someone's question) First time we met."

D: "I named my son for you . . . and Eddy Arnold (Merle Arnold Watson)"

M: "That's what I heard. I appreciate that."

D: "I figured a little of that good guitar pickin' might rub off on him"

M: "Look who's talkin' . . . Hey, that guitar rings like a bell!"

D: "Pretty good old box . . . yeah, Mr. Gallagher made this thing. Lives down near Wartrace, Tennessee."

M: "Granpa Jones got one."

D: "You know, in my opinion one of the finest albums you ever did? Think about it just a minute . . . think about what I might like"

M: "That first old 78 thing?"

Doc and Merle first meeting

D: "That was a good album . . . beautiful album. Right along the top . . . but it wasn't my favorite."

M: "Well, I have no idea . . ."

D: "You remember the thing that your brother had a whole lot to do with writing?"

M: "Ohhh, that old coal mine thing?"

D: "That's a fine album . . . I thought once you came up and shook hands I'd say 'hello, second-cousin Claude . . . I'm proud I got a copy of that . . . coal miner's songs . . . in mint condition just about—there might be a couple of dust scratches on it. I think I'm gonna put it on a tape, in case somethin' happens to it."

M: "Good God. They wanted me to do that . . . every song in that that thing, I made it up in two weeks."

D: "Yeah! And what one helluva job you did!"

M: "Now I can say that you and me are buddies"

D: "Officially, we have met!"

M: "People always say 'do you know Doc Watson (he says Watkins here)? I say I never got to meet him."

Bill comes into the studio and "interrupts":

Bill: "Now, we have Dobro, five string . . ."

M: "I'll see you after a while."

Doc: "We'll talk some more . . . let's go right in to it. . . leave it roll . . ."

Then he started the definitive version of "Way Downtown."

What was amazing was that it worked out as planned: Doc Watson would be getting ready to record and in would walk Merle Travis, to finally meet him and talk a bit! Doc had named his son after Merle—and Eddy Arnold (Merle Eddy Watson)—and had, as exhibited here (and on the album) the highest respect for him one could have. They talk about records, favorite songs, and the guitar Doc plays made by "Mr. Gallagher down in Wartrace, Tennessee."

Merle's entrance caught us off guard, as we were getting ready to record "Way Downtown" in a few minutes, but that could wait now!

Two music giants

Travis begins talking, fifteen feet away from the nearest mic. I had to interrupt him to position a mic close to his mouth so we could hear him on the tape. (You can hear some of this on the recording.) Bill and I had this planned out, and I was to help make it work, glad I was there to capture this most important exchange between these two music giants. The air or atmosphere around them was like they had met many times and just had not seen each other for a while.

Listeners should know they were amazed at the attention given to them for their music over the years. There was not any competition visible, or evident, between them, though. They got along just fine from the first words of greeting. Merle was genuinely surprised that Doc knew so much about his music, and Doc felt the same about what Merle knew about him. They had not lived that far apart. Muhlenberg County, Kentucky (where Travis started), is about 430 miles from Deep Gap, Doc's home. But in those early days, it was a long way to go to look for someone. By the time Doc would have become interested and able, Travis had moved to the West Coast. That lasted until the 1960s, when Merle made the move to Nashville, and Doc was off working in various situations.

Junior Huskey: Hands on Bass

Earl took Bill and me to the Opry the week prior to recording *Circle* (the day prior to rehearsing) to meet the bass player he had arranged, Junior Huskey. We strolled in backstage with Earl in the lead, and Bill and I with hair that Dolly Parton would have wanted. Earl said "hi" to the guard, and those beautiful words "they're with me . . . ," that got us in. The inquisitive looks we received from the Opry people on the stage were somewhat strange (the players who are coming up to perform next were all around, waiting their turn, in fine dresses and sequined suits—"stars") but more curious because Earl's sons also had long hair. They didn't know why we were there.

We walked out on to the stage with the show going on to meet Junior Huskey, but he couldn't shake hands right then because he was playing while someone in front was singing. Junior was playing along with him, while saying to us "I'm really lookin' forward to pickin' with y'all. I cut my teeth on these tunes. I'm ready to pick. Just a minute, please," as he looked out on center stage a

Roy "Junior" Huskey

few feet away to watch the guy ending the song and grabbed the final two notes of that song with him. He was accompanying Hank Snow singing "I'm Movin' On," while chatting with us! "Hey, this guy's good" I thought.

We knew Earl had picked the right man! Bill had wanted to make sure the bass would be nailed down and right. We knew then it would be. After Junior passed twenty years later, his son, Roy Huskey, Jr., played on recordings with me (*String Wizards* and *String Wizards II* on Vanguard Records) and did the same great job with his dad's bass.

Junior didn't say much during the sessions, but when he did it was usually funny in his dry way. One day he was shaking a maraca and listening to it and then said, whispering to us, "Hey, one of you guys should tell the engineer (shakes maraca again) something's broken in this thing." Or, when he quietly said to Jeff, "Hey, Jeff! When Maybelle sings that verse about the hearse comin' to get her mama, get that washboard out and make an old car sound, like a back-firing sound . . . that would help it out, I think!" On that one we had another much-needed laugh, putting us at ease a bit before recording it.

I noticed his attitude could put others at ease, too, so they could concentrate on the music. I did not hear one mistake on bass the whole week! He knew the songs before we did and was a good one to listen to when running through the songs, and he helped us get them. Doc even complimented him on "Tennessee Stud," saying "that is about as pretty a bass line I've heard played on somethin' in a long time. I compliment that boy back there."

Earl had made the right choice for many reasons, one being that Junior had played with most of the people on the Opry (he was staff bass player there) before at some point, putting them at ease. And it was letting Les rest from the bass chores to concentrate on mandolin. Earl's perfect choices would become obvious again with Vassar.

Jeff and Snare Drum

Jeff was a natural drummer. His wrists and hands were excellent with brushes, and he did the "train thing" just right, which was perfect for some of the tunes. Snare, high hat, bass drum (not always used) filled a space no one else was playing in. It was the only drums we had on the sessions and in the right hands. He knew the importance to keeping time and, in my mind, it made it sound more traditional. Ibby played snare also, and it is hard to tell who is playing just by listening because they both did great. The light snare fit right in with some of the Travis songs, and on some of the songs

Jeff Hanna

one of them might not be singing on. They would be the "designated drummer." We did not use drums on many songs, either.

The bluegrass I had listened to sometimes had a guy on brushes, hitting the snare drum. Jimmie Fadden realized we needed the harp and wasn't really playing drums a lot yet, and we needed the harp. Jeff had played drums on a couple of NGDB songs just a few years earlier, and now he was reliving being a part of that sound. I always felt good if Jeff or Ibby was on snare. They didn't drag, and you could count on them.

In Jeff's case, snare was a substitute for his washboard. There's more to the washboard than meets the fingers, and he scraped a lot of sounds from it. "Thimbles on his fingers would make the noise," dragging on the washboard plate, hitting the bell, wood blocks (attached to it); sometimes, he would just click the thimbles on the metal. Jeff especially shined with it on "Nashville Blues."

Les Thompson's Mandolin

Les played bass and mandolin with NGDB and sang whenever he could. His mandolin playing was patterned after Dean Webb from the Dillards, whom he admired and followed in his younger years. We both followed, literally, the Dillards. Les was also influenced by Roland White (fantastic guitarist Clarence White was his younger brother), who played around the LA area and did the Saturday morning car sales show (Cal Worthington had bluegrass on while he sold cars!) and the hot Kentucky Colonels—they were great.

Bill got a great shot of Les's hands, and a lot of people have asked me "who is the mandolin player in that photo?" It's Les! I am not sure what song he is playing; I think he was just practicing. It shows him doing that tremolo at which he was so good. I told him I was always (to this day), jealous of his tremolo! It was better than mine.

Les has told me recently what a shock it was to him, to be playing with Earl and Doc and Jimmy Martin, and Travis because he was just getting it going a few years earlier. And with our band (the Moonshiners) together before NGDB, he sang and played guitar. He "practiced up" for these

Les Thompson

sessions! His playing on "Way Downtown" and "Nashville Blues" was just what the songs called for, and under pressure, he delivered.

Les left the band around 1975, a nine-year run, and then ran a successful goldsmith business in the Washington, DC area. In 2015 I called him to see if he would want to play with me again, and there we were, fifty years after the first time, playing together again. In all those years, we have never had a bad word between us.

Jeff Learns a Lick from Doc

While working on the harmony part for "Way Downtown" Jeff was in a space he never dreamed of as a teenager picking at McCabe's . . . well, maybe dreamed of, but did not think it possible: to record with Doc Watson. I was working on the frailing banjo part and not listening to this conversation as they ran it down, but, as he is with all his harmony work, Jeff wanted to get it right. Just like Doc would want is what we all strived for, not realizing he already was doing the job.

Doc's pickin' was on fire, and he tore it up. Doc calling the solos out (who was to play next) was the fun part because it made it feel like a picking party caught live. His incredible guitar fills need to be noted between lines of the song because all that guitar was Doc himself.

Jeff Hanna and Doc Watson

The Great Jimmy Martin

We had never met anyone like him. We will most likely not meet anyone who comes close. Jimmy Martin, the self-proclaimed "King of Bluegrass" lived up to his title. He was an energetic, nice, opinionated man, demanding the rhythm be right and the vocals good. Real good. He brought us up to his level, with instructions as to singing, phrasing, and picking. We could not have had a better teacher, and he kept pushing us to do better—until we did good enough.

The great Jimmy Martin

Jimmy was excited to record "Sunny Side of the Mountain," one of his signature songs, and get it on this album. I was excited to play it, be part of a real bluegrass band (as real as we ever have been), and to hold down J. D. Crowe's part on the song. I guess I passed the "Martin exam" because at the end of the recording as we headed in to listen to the playback, Jimmy says, "You got all them banjo breaks in your head, hain't cha, John . . . you're gettin' all of them." It felt good getting that high of a compliment from him.

Henry C. McAuliffe and Bobby Gregory brought out this song first in 1944, but Jimmy gave it a new life, making it sound like it was his song. He would do that with many songs he sang, like Linda Ronstadt would. (She thought highly of him as a singer.) Jimmy's "Hold Whatcha Got" (on *Circle III*) was another fine example of "owning" a song he wrote—well, all of them were. J. D. Crowe told me Jimmy made him do that single-string approach he used on the song . . . very clever, that.

Bill and I used to do "You Don't Know My Mind" when, in those pre-NGDB years, we went on stage together and never thought we would meet the King of Bluegrass. When NGDB did that song on the album, with Bill producing it, it was a dream come true for me to be replicating J. D. Crowe again.

Jimmy's songs were to the point, as when I was inducting him into the Bluegrass Hall of Fame. Orin Friesen (who was running the induction in 1995) asked me to talk with him about what I was going to say about him. It was fun, and he was adamant about one thing. He said "Just make sure you tell them I tell it like it is . . . like I feel it . . . like my new song about my new ex-wife . . . It's called 'I Shouldn't Have Said I Do, But I Did.'"

The King of Bluegrass

He came from Sneedville, Tennessee, and had played with some of the greats. Jimmy Martin was also one of the greats who would willingly show us the way. Earl's wife, Louise Scruggs, lined him up and told me later she had said to Jimmy, "If you mess this one up, I won't talk to you for a long time. . . . Just keep your mouth shut." It had been known by those "on the inside" that Martin put the color in bluegrass. He would talk a lot in his shows between songs, but for *Circle* he was "tamed" a bit, as I found out later from Louise.

In 1949 Martin became lead vocalist for Bill Monroe's "Blue Grass Boys." Martin's high voice mixing with Monroe's tenor came to be known as the "high lonesome" sound. Martin challenged Monroe to raise the pitch on many of his classics and to write new, "lonesome" songs. Martin's lead was defining in "lonesome" songs such as "Memories of Mother and Dad" and "I'm Blue, I'm Lonesome."

Jimmy Martin

Jimmy's famously high-strung and exuberant personality was known at the time by all but us. We would find out later. He inevitably clashed with Monroe's equally tenacious temperament, leaving Monroe to work briefly with the Osborne Brothers, until he formed his own band, the Sunny Mountain Boys, in 1955. He credited himself with inventing the "G" run—the guitar lick used widely in the bluegrass. However, record evidence from the period before Martin began performing professionally clearly shows Lester Flatt using this run when backing Bill Monroe (Flatt and Earl played with Monroe in 1945).

The week before the sessions, showing up for rehearsal at Martin's house was my "becoming J. D. Crowe" moment, as I had to channel one of the big influencers on me. He had picked banjo (and sang) many years with Jimmy as a member of the Sunny Mountain Boys.

Martin greeted us at his front door with cheerful exuberance, and said, after about two minutes of introduction, "You know, they won't let me on the Opry anymore! I went over too good. Here . . . lemme play you my last time at the Opry." He cued up a waiting tape to run a song, or so we thought. Well, it was about two minutes of the applause after his last song, no music. He kept saying over it to us "that's what they think of Jimmy Martin there . . . at the Grand Ole Opry!! That's what they did for me! That crowd ate me up! And they won't let me on again!"

Jeff and Ibby sang bluegrass with one of the greats and held their own; they did a fine job. Jimmy would have told them if they hadn't because that was his way. Kind of like when he commented on my playing on the first song, "Earl never did do that!" When I hit a big "clam" (musician mistake), Bill kept it in the record . . . the first thing you hear.

Rehearsals were great. Jimmy was fun and seemed to be just a few years older in attitude, although he was much older in age. I had the best rhythm guitarist picking behind me ever. "Sunny Side of the Mountain" made me feel like all those hours listening to J. D. were paying off. I thought this might make it possible to meet Crowe someday. (That happened a few years later, when I recorded with him on a Larry Rice record. I was frailing to his picking and we became friends.) I went to see J. D. in Lexington, Kentucky, at the Holiday Inn, well after the *Circle*, late in the 1970s for that session. There was not a large crowd there. In fact, it was about twenty-three normal-sized people. During a break (I believe he had left Martin a year earlier and was trying to get his own thing going), sitting at a table, he said "John, this bluegrass thing isn't workin' so well. I been thinkin' . . . I'm a gonna get one of those Fender twin reverb amps, a wah-wah pedal, an' plug in m' banjer, an' go get some of that money." Fortunately, his following grew over a few years, and he kept playing, some of the best bluegrass out there, with his band New South. He didn't get the amp and always said, "Jimmy drove me in to it."

At the studio, Martin was anxious and getting ready to pick. He just seemed excited and eager to record. I did not realize we were "stars" to him. We had been performing at that time only about five years; he had been in it since the1940s. In the previous year, we had three *Billboard*-charting songs, but Bill and I had been listening to his music and playing it for a couple of years. He was "Jimmy Martin, King of Bluegrass, the best bluegrass singer in the world" (as he introduced himself to anyone) and was the star to us.

He chatted it up with Vassar, whom I would learn later was "tolerating" him quite well (I added some of their chatter on the remastered *Circle* album). They had played together often, and although Vassar played on his albums, he did not get credit. He was a sideman, but here they were on equal turf. Jimmy had spent several years as a sideman with other groups, so he related to Vassar on that level, too.

"Losin' You," the first cut, went great! The guys sang great, and we were playing bluegrass! I was playing in F without a capo, doing all right, and getting the licks in every hole, the way Jimmy liked it.

"Sunny Side of the Mountain" was wonderful to do, and I felt like one of the Sunny Mountain Boys with Vassar, Junior, and Martin's Martin on rhythm. I had to pick hard, very hard! So hard, I pulled the first two strings out of the bridge and had to get a new bridge, and I broke a *metal* fingerpick!

Then came "My Walkin' Shoes," my least favorite "execution." My banjo was just not sharp enough, and I thought it sounded like folky banjo more than bluegrass, plodding along instead sprightly picking. But it worked, sounded different, and the singers worked well. Ibby and Les were having a great time singing, and Jeff realized "this guy" he had not heard of was pretty damn good! Fadden pairing his harp up with Vassar was going to work great. Vassar loved it, he said.

Then came the "Grand Ole Opry Song," which took some convincing. Jimmy said (when Bill suggested it to him) "well, Bill, a lot of those people are . . . dead!" Bill told him we were honoring them, and Martin liked that. It was to be the opening cut, like it had been written for this album. I got to play in C with regular tuning (without capo). It is the one I fumbled, for which I am so glad because if I had not, Jimmy would not have uttered what became famous in the bluegrass world: "Earl never did do that . . . pick it solid, John. You been pickin' one for fifteen years, hadn't ya?" Everyone laughed! I thought it had only been seven years. We launched into it and, like the others, got it in one take. I made a mistake on that one smack in the middle of the song. I wish it was not there, but it goes by so fast I don't think it is heard.

When we got to the Hank Williams song "I Saw the Light" with Acuff, Martin made a point, pulling us aside, "I'm gointa sing this so much like Acuff you won't be able to tell us apart!" He was right. Not sure which verse Martin did to this day.

I think my best cut with Jimmy was "You Don't Know My Mind," where I got to play that fourth-string lead like J. D. It reminds every time when I was hanging out in the dressing room (the damp basement at the Golden Bear in 1965) to learn from the Dillards. Douglas Dillard went up those stairs, he played that lick, and looked at me with that silly grin of his, saying, "J. D. Crowe. Go check him out. Plays with Jimmy Martin."

Martin's Phrasing

Getting it right so the "King of Bluegrass" would be happy about it was important to the singers on "Losin' You (Might Be the Best Thing Yet)." Working on smoothing out the vocals was best done without headphones because you could hear what was being sung in the room and blend together better.

Vassar's kickoff (he is just to the left of Les) and Fadden's harp worked great as support to the vocals. The banjo playing high notes against the low guitar, with the fiddle doing the "textures" of the lyrics, made the perfect arrangement of the band. Martin's phrasing of "might be" coming out more like "maht be" had to be matched by the singers, which they also did with "thing," making it more like "thang."

L–R: Les Thompson, Jimmy Ibbotson, Jeff Hanna, Jimmy Martin, John McEuen

Martin's phrasing on "quite a name" was something he did best, putting in some of his personality, and made sense in this recording. And when he sang "the life you chosed," it seemed like the right word at the right time, even though it is not in the English language! It was in Martin's language. "Everythang" Martin did was perfect to me on the whole album, and the guys knew working with him was a privilege they did not take for granted. He was adamant about recording his music right, and his bass licks (on guitar) fit right in just right.

Norman Blake

Born in Chattanooga, Tennessee, and raised in Alabama, Norman Blake was playing guitar by the time he reached eleven years old. When he dropped out of school at sixteen, he didn't take it easy but went on to learn mandolin, Dobro, fiddle, more guitar, and worked at all of them. He played music then to earn money, and a couple of years later went to the Army. After an Army stint he moved to Nashville where Blake became a top session musician and was in the studio when Bob Dylan came to town to record with the studio musicians dubbed the "Nashville cats." Norman worked with Johnny Cash over a period of thirty years and spent time fishing with Cash and playing music as part of Cash's House Band on the Johnny Cash summer television show.

Foreground: Norman Blake, Background: Jimmy Fadden, Vassar Clements

Norman Blake, Jimmie McFadden, Vassar Clements

"Togary Mountain"

I was "driving the bus" on "Togary Mountain," recording "an old bluegrass tune" that I had just made up, taking from a few sources I wanted to honor. Bill took the session photo and did some things to it to make it look as old-time as possible.

It had only been eight weeks since asking Earl, Doc, and Travis those questions, and here we were recording real music with real people. It made me think of that night at Tulagi, after asking Doc if he would record, and he said "yes." I drove home and could not sleep that night. Whew! Our idol was going to record with the Dirt Band! I called Bill from home, and he said, "I think I'll get Merle Travis." It was starting.

Now, we were going to record with the NGDB, Vassar, Norman Blake, and Junior Huskey; we were finally "Nashville cats." We were on the way!

"Togary Mountain" This photo was aged by Bill McEuen where he inserted the original WSM radio station mixing board from 1936. This was Bill's "secret." See original photo on page 92.

Vassar's God's Head Fiddle

I had met John Harford after Chet Atkins suggested he add the "t" to his name, so people could remember it better. It was when he was playing the banjo on the *Glen Campbell Show* and around the time of "Gentle on My Mind" (which he wrote), and he was doing fine. He told me he took his first royalty check to use for a down payment on an LA apartment complex that he renamed as a joke Marvin Gardens.

I didn't know then he would give a fiddle, which is seen here in Vassar's hands, to Clements. It became his instrument, that sweet sounding and loud instrument seemed made for Vassar and his music, letting him go anywhere he ventured. Some thought it was partly that fiddle with the carved head that possessed some kind of special magic that drew notes from a place we were not in, a place where the "magic notes" were stored and kept until the right person came along to check some of them out.

The story I heard from Marty Stuart was that Hartford was trying to get better in the late 1960s with his fiddling and not having much success. John had acquired that fiddle with the carved head, and after a while, frustrated, gave it to Vassar. Vassar was just coming out of drinking and did not have a fiddle, and he went to making sweet music with his new (old) special instrument. Hartford

Vassar Clements's fiddle head

then said, a few months later, that his own playing was improving, as if by some miracle. Giving away the fiddle to Vassar, he figured, must have done that.

Hearing Vassar play later on other fiddles the notes came from him. I was complaining about how my fiddle just seemed to squawk a bit too much one day, and some of the notes did not seem true. I handed it to Vassar to play. It sounded fine. I quit squawking and practiced my troubles away; about two years later it had improved.

It wasn't his Florida upbringing, nor his apprenticeship with Monroe and others, as he signed on wherever he went to be a full-time player, although not getting credit as a sideman. It was him. Bill gave him the credit on *Circle* that he so rightly deserved. Thanks to Earl for bringing him to us!

VASSAR CLEMENTS's RING

The ring on this hand is for the one Vassar always later said, "I'll have to check with Millie," his wife and manager for so many years. She looked out for him, booked him, and handled business things.

Vassar Clements's Ring

Louise Scruggs was a perfect example and mentor for Millie and a force in the music community of Nashville at the time. Louise managed Earl (and previously Flatt & Scruggs) and, to my knowledge, was the one who kept it all together for him. She made the calls, the deals, the concepts for albums, titles for albums, chose photography, and did all that work necessary for "a banjo player's wife" to do. Earl was not "just a banjo player."

Vassar's hand here is showing how perfect his notation was, as his fingers are all close together and working the neck and close to the neck waiting for the next note. His fingers never "flew around" nor was the pinky ever straight up in the air when not being used. They were all down close to the fingerboard, waiting for action.

His fiddle was loud and, in my opinion, easy to play because I tried it out a couple of times and handed it back fairly quickly. It did seem, feel-wise, to be a bit of a more "adult" fiddle. I had only been playing a few years at the time of *Circle*, worked with it a lot of hours on NGDB music, so I could get it as right as I could. Never anything intricate, but basic fiddle that worked well with our songs. Vassar was from a different planet and took it to spaces I never knew a fiddle could go. Now, I know; I just can't get there myself.

Finding "Togary Mountain"

One late October night in 1970 young Gary Scruggs, after playing the *Uncle Charlie* album for his dad, asked him if he would "like to go see that band that did 'Randy Lynn Rag'?" Earl's enthusiastic "yes" put them all on the path to Vanderbilt a couple of weeks later. I owned every Flatt & Scruggs album available on the West Coast and had spent a lot of time learning his tunes, slowing down the instrumentals to 16⅔ speed to figure out the notes. I was introduced to the Carter Family music through them. Earl was definitely my idol!

I had met Merle Watson in LA earlier in the year at a concert with his father, Doc Watson, but it was too crowded to meet Doc. It was an after-show music-pickin' party; everyone trying to get Doc's attention or play their notes for him . . . all that kind of thing. I watched. Since NGDB was not thought highly of in those circles, I decided to hang in the background. I went to shy Merle instead, met him, and told him my plan. He had played Doc the *Uncle Charlie* album, he told me!

The next week Doc Watson was to play at Tulagi's! Now, as I had planned, I could ask Doc the same question, telling him Earl was to record with us. I would be able to play on "Tennessee Stud," "Way Downtown," and music I loved—"Soldier's Joy" in particular—with Earl!

"Togary Mountain" rehearsal

I arrived at Doc's Colorado concert a few months later and excitedly told Merle "Earl said yes!" Merle responded, "I'd better introduce you to Daddy. I played him that *Uncle Charlie* album, an' he 'specially liked 'Clinch Mt. Backstep' [one with banjo and Les's mandolin with the band. Merle and Doc lived around Ralph Stanley's Clinch Mountain area, which I did not know.] . . . I'm sure he'll do it, too. He needs this, as the folk music 'thing' has been winding down lately." Just what I wanted to hear.

An hour later, meeting with Doc, I told him the story of what I wanted to do: get Earl together with him and the NGDB and make some recordings. He loved the idea, saying "If Earl's goin' to be there, I want to pick too."

Now it was time for "the Big Gun." I called our manager. After putting him on the phone with Bill (from Tulagi's dressing room—young club manager Chuck Morris, knowing the importance of this meeting, dug up a fifty-foot cord for the phone to run up to the dressing room), Bill's

"Togary Mountain" recording

knowledge of "old music," Delta blues, and of Doc himself impressed him, and he agreed to do it. We were on the way! It was starting.

Fast-forward to rehearsal week at Earl's house two months later, last week of July 1971. A chuckling Louise told me one night, after playing all day, "That "Randy Lynn Rag" . . . every time Earl and Flatt would do that on TV or whatever, little Gary would get up and stomp out of the room, saying 'Daddy never wrote a song for me!'"

I had an instrumental to record on the album but did not have a name for it yet. So, on the *Circle* album this one of mine is "To Gary Mountain," which I changed to "Togary Mountain." Gary had a song named after him at last!

I had just finished "Soldier's Joy" with Earl, which had been one goal—to record that song, with me frailing and Earl picking, and just Junior's bass, and now, with "Togary Mountain," I was recording with the NGDB and Vassar, Norman Blake, and Junior—real Nashville cats.

Norman Blake was hot on the Dobro, playing I believe what the missing Josh Graves would have done. I had admired Norman since that time and especially proud that years later the *O Brother, Where Art Thou?* soundtrack on which he appeared (the *Circle* is often referred to as the "father" of *O Brother*) had done so very well. I am glad Earl had his number.

Also on "Togary's" second banjo solo, I got pay tribute to Douglas Flint Dillard, my original inspiration to pick in the first place. What I played on that part is a direct steal (let's call it an homage) of what he played on Liberty, on the first *Dillards Back Porch Bluegrass* album, a record that changed my life.

Vassar Clements

In the weeks prior to recording, some small details had to be figured out: who some of the players would be. I asked Earl if he could find some fiddlers to cover some of the different styles represented on the album to be, and he said over the phone, "I found one man—Vassar Clements." To which I foolishly asked, "Can he cover all the music?" Earl's gently emphatic firm answer of "He'll do" put the icing on that fiddle cake.

Kissimee fiddle

I had heard Vassar on countless recordings by Bill Monroe (he was with him seven years), Jim and Jesse McReynolds, Jimmy Martin, and others but did not know it. Those albums never had credits, reserving all the print for the "stars" making the records. We would quickly learn he was from another planet!

Here he is seen in a rare situation, looking at his strings. When he played, Vassar usually was looking around the room, into space, or somewhere he was finding those magic notes to play, notes that made people want to pick up the fiddle and try it for themselves.

Jeff and Maybelle Carter

Jeff, like all of us, loved the Carter Family's music, but none of us realized how so much of it came from Maybelle until after the *Circle* sessions. The guitar style, the keys, a lot of the arrangements, the vocals that she delivered were all a huge influence on so many, and credit came to the family for all of it. It is funny the Carter Scratch is not called "Maybelle's Scratch," as she was the only one playing guitar in that manner.

Dino Lappas, Bill McEuen (back turned) and Maybelle Carter

Maybelle Carter and Jeff Hanna

The reach of her music might have been best said by Duane Allman's daughter, on a phone call I had with her around 2004. She was commenting about how, one night when she was little, her dad taught her mom how to play "Wildwood Flower" on the guitar. She remembered it as a sweet moment. I thought about, as she was telling me about her father, Duane ("the greatest guitarist in the world"—*Rolling Stone* magazine) knew of Maybelle and how she played and knew some of her music. What an impact she did have!!

Jeff was going to sing with Maybelle on this song. He knew "up close and personal" was the best way to work it out. I wondered what was going through his mind as he sat at the feet of the fountain of country music and tapped into her flow.

Maybelle, if she was just standing there and one did not know her, was like a "fine woman who might've had some talent . . . for sewing or cooking," but put a guitar in her hands (or autoharp) and if you let her, she would show you the direction country music was headed for the next many years.

The Source

What the heck are we doing in this photo? Merle Travis next to Oswald Kirby next to (partially seen) Earl Scruggs, all backing up Jeff and Maybelle Carter singing "Thinking Tonight of My Blue Eyes." That this song was used at least twice to make other country music hits—the same melody with different words—suggests the power this simple music had. Maybelle makes it her own with this great capturing of her guitar style, a style that is often emulated by beginning guitarists as part of what one needs to learn.

"The Source," Mother Maybelle Carter, Merle Travis, Oswald Kirby, Jeff Hanna

Mother Maybelle

Jeff was at his reverent best, sitting in front of Mother Maybelle, someone we were not sure was even still alive in 1965, when us pre-NGDB teens were discovering music of old times. It was called folk music and spoke of a different era, in a longing fashion, of places distant and appealing. It seemed to be ancient times where those songs came from and was not from anyone we knew. We were all California kids at this time (from different places, our parents all came, to call SoCal home), and well ensconced in the life of no disasters or strife, the life of "good American kids." We did not have mining cave-ins, train wrecks, banjos in the hollow, murdered pregnant girlfriends, a willow tree we wanted to be buried under, relatives lost in floods, fires, and we weren't worried about a "Tom Dooley," but we wanted to sing and play about those things and people because it made us feel important.

Then each of us found, through different channels, our way to Carter Family music—music of olden times long gone, as (apparently) the people were. We wished they were around to be seen and heard in other forms than on a record. Then, the folk boom happened within our generation. We found out! They were still here! The people were still around, and now Jeff was at the feet of a woman who was recording before Black Tuesday and whose musical family thrived as the market crashed, things we had only briefly heard about in school.

We were the generation that was being primed for Vietnam, still in the fuzzy future, as we learned our trade. We didn't pay close attention to Vietnam yet, not wanting to go was about it. We were all trying to do something crazy: to make a living with music.

You could not deny that Maybelle was living in a different world, playing from a different playbook, where keeping on the sunny side was actually done; where death and life were addressed head-on and dealt with, where there seemed to be hope for all as would appear in the lyrics to "Will the Circle Be Unbroken," "There's a better place a-waiting, by and by."

The Wrap-up of the Circle

It was finally time for the "Circle" song, as we all gathered in the studio to run it down. I don't know what I was saying to Acuff, but everyone was in a good mood. It had been a great week, with

L–R: Earl Scruggs, John McEuen, Vassar Clements, Roy Acuff, foreground left Maybelle Carter

thirty-six songs being recorded, and we were just about done. The blond with the beautiful smile is Bill's wife Alice, who, along with everyone who wanted to be there at the sessions, became one of the singers of "Circle." Bill would later entice her to do the calligraphy for the credits on the album, written out in her beautiful handwriting. It would look great, but a problem arose.

Bill's artistic mind told him the credits (NGDB players and featured guest players—"stars") should be on the cover, put on parchment paper, and needed to have a little "burnish" to them, color—like age—something that today would be done in Photoshop. This led to creating a difficult situation for him, or more for her, because to get the desired effect with the parchment she did the writing on, he put it on a flat pan in the oven, and let it set for a while. Too long of a while, it was. Her two days of lettering work caught fire and burned up too much. But it was so beautiful, he talked her in to doing it a second time; this time, he baked it at a lower temperature for this "credit toasting," and it came out great.

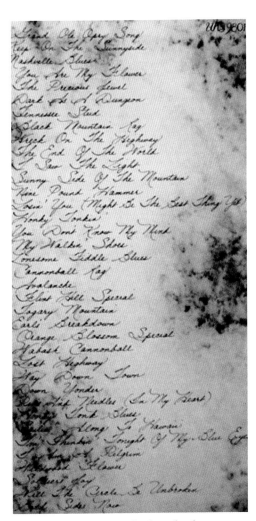

Alice McEuen calligraphy from back cover

While Earl and Vassar tuned, Maybelle is watching Roy, and it was just before this she said something to the effect of "Roy, it sure is good to record with you. All these years, and we have never done anything together!" Roy agreed and was glad to be there; we continued to get ready.

Junior is seen in the dark area between Vassar and Acuff, hanging on his bass as he normally would, watching Travis and Doc (out of the frame), all from his bass perch. It seems he was focused on Dino this time, as Dino adjusts a mic. Dino was meticulous, and by then, he and we all knew whatever this was we were creating, it would be well captured and around for a long time as a record of an event we would not want to leave nor forget. It would be music to the ears of thousands of folks out there, a salve for the soul, a coming together of the ages, in a space where time stood still, with no agenda other than "get it right the first time."

It was the best of times in the midst of a most difficult time in the United States. It was a time when the country had gone through recent assassinations, churches were being burned, the Kent State massacre was still fresh in memory, political parties never seemed so far apart, and the president was lying to his people. Some things do not change . . . sometimes. It was the dawning of an old era, a hearkening to the past, bringing it back, once again.

Dino and the Control Room

We had just finished the first one of Roy Acuff's songs "Wreck on the Highway," and he had to hear it. Pausing to listen back was always a special time to us, as you could listen to the "finished product" from the other room. If you could hear everything—through the closed control room doors, hearing it muffled in the studio—or hearing headphone leakage from a bunch of headphone sets laying around (their previous users were in the control room, listening), and pick out all the licks and hear the vocals and the words of the lead singer; well, you knew it was a good mix. But staying out of that pressure in the control room and avoiding each other's eyes as the music played because it might not be right.

Earl was enjoying it immensely, and Oswald had never heard his Dobro so well. (He told me that he liked it that loud on backup licks; that was Bill's mixing.) Acuff was loving it, not showing it yet, but he was listening intently. We were on pins and needles waiting for it to be over to get their reaction—Acuff's reaction—and hopefully, approval.

L–R: Earl Scruggs, Roy Acuff, Oswald Kirby, Dino Lappas

After giving the "big" guys their time to listen, if they approved the cut we went in to hear it again with them, too. It would then sound great on the warm studio speakers, full volume, and roaring away. There were a lot of playbacks that week!

This was a real test for audio mixer Dino Lappas, who Bill had flown in from LA to engineer the sessions. Dino had worked on two of our albums prior to this one and was the head engineer for Liberty Records at the time, working at Third Street Recorders on the south edge of Hollywood. Dino had worked with the Ventures and the Jazz Crusaders and on Glen Campbell's twelve-string guitar records and countless others, including a lot of World Pacific Jazz records (a label that made unusual recordings). But, most important to me, he did the Dillards' *Back Porch Bluegrass* album (on Electra Records) in that same studio in which NGDB cut, six years later, *Uncle Charlie*. The band all had a good time working with him, and though he had an air of authority, he knew what to do to get the sound on the tape he chose. You could trust him. And, he put up with a bunch of kids who barely knew what to do at the time. He had seen us grow in the studio and was proud to be there. Dino had to keep the setups in order, be ready to record various types of songs, log them right, and he put order to the day. Bill learned a lot from him while we played!

Getting Ready to "Keep on the Sunny Side"

Randy, Travis, Les, Ibby, Gary, Junior, Mother Maybelle, Jimmie, and Doc (Jeff's back is visible; he is wearing the striped shirt).

No one was even looking at Mother Maybelle, and it is strange that there are five different groups of things going in this moment, as seen here. We are getting ready to record "Keep on the Sunny Side." Jimmie Fadden and Doc are in their own world, while Les, Ibby, and Gary are in theirs. Travis is talking to Junior about old things, old sessions, old records. Jeff, seen here in the striped shirt, is waiting to get Maybelle's attention about words they are to sing. Randy is tuning the mandolin, and all are in that groove of life that will make a great recording.

The Circle gathers

In the same way that one waits for the sun to rise, in the moments just before it becomes visible, then the magic happens that is the sunrise, that is what it was like in this room. You knew the sun was coming up with "Keep on the Sunny Side." You knew that some magic was going to happen, and you knew that everybody had a part to do.

What we didn't know yet was Maybelle tuned her guitar a half-step flat, so when she was playing in C, she was actually in C-flat. She did not tune the autoharp down, though, saying it would be in "F-natural." I didn't know it meant that until forty years later, when I started working with John Carter Cash, her grandson, and he explained it to me.

Everyone felt the sense of the importance with Maybelle. After all, she was Maybelle Carter of the Carter Family, and she helped create country music. But when Marty Stuart and I took her the gold record with her name on, she said, "I didn't realize that many people had heard these old songs. Do you boys want some lemonade?" as she set it down against a wall. She said she would put it in the "music room," a medium-sized room where people came to play on Friday or Saturday nights after an Opry show. (I wrote a song called "Friday Night at Maybelle's" in honor of that on *String Wizards*)

Keep on the Sunny Side

With Doc, Oswald, Earl, Junior, Vassar, Maybelle, Chet Flippo (from *Rolling Stone*, who did an article for the magazine about the sessions), NGDB (Jeff, Ibby, Les, and me), Gary Scruggs, and Travis all joining for the "other" signature Maybelle Carter song, "Keep on the Sunny Side," how could we go wrong? It was a great moment, frozen in time for all, starting with Doc asking her if she remembered "the old ending you put on that thing" gave us her intro of "on that old record I started it like this," and then she started it. It was like a script. It was like a dream, as we were all transported back to 1927 Bristol, Tennessee, when she, A. P. Carter and Sarah first recorded this benchmark song, starting country music.

Before we started, I asked if she was going to "stay tuned like that for all the things were doing in here," because she tuned down one fret on the guitar, so her D chord was actually Db! She thought it made the guitar sound better. (I think it made it "meatier," gave it that real "Maybelle" sound.)

Maybelle, prior to this starting song, asked if she could do "Wildwood Flower" on the autoharp; she said, "if y'all don't mind. I've never recorded it on the autoharp. I done it with the guitar about

Circle together

a dozen times. And I do it in F—standard. And I'll try to do it in F Standard key on the autoharp. And, ahhh, 'Thinking Tonight of My Blue Eyes.' I'll have to do in the same place. And then, I don't know where we'll do 'Will the Circle Be Unbroken.' If everybody sings, get a key that suits everybody." It's on the record, this magic moment.

We ran through it a couple of times before recording, and Vassar was playing all over it, as he got bored on such a simple song and had to see what he could do. Maybelle called out to him at the end of the second rehearsal and said, "Vassar Clements, could you just play the melody, and quit all that foolin' around when we record?" Vassar shyly promptly said, "ahhh, yes Mama Maybelle, jus' seein' what the fiddle could do."

Listen to the last chord and think about all those people in the studio being quiet. It took about eight seconds for her ending guitar lick to die out and shows what a great recording process Bill had set up with recording it at thirty inches per second (ips) and the two-track process.

Chet Flippo's article would appear in *Rolling Stone* and by special permission be one of the sleeves with the album package. Chet did a lot for this music in getting the word out. Thank you, Mr. Flippo. I spoke at his memorial and told him then.

Break Time for the Nashville Cats

While tape was being changed, it gave the Nashville cats a chance to visit and talk about things, other musicians, or just life. Each reel of tape was good for four or five songs, or three times through a song, then another one more tune. At thirty inches per second, a lot of tape was eaten up in the process, and the reels had to be changed about every thirty to forty-five minutes. You did not want to run out of tape before the end of the song, especially when it was the master! Two-track tape was much less expensive than multitrack and easier to keep track of, so there were many reasons to record two-track. Our $22,000 budget for the record was just enough.

You can see the pride Earl had for Randy (as he had for Gary and Steve) when he looks at him, sitting with his peers, at seventeen years old. Randy was the "hot" guitar picker at the time and played beyond his age and expected abilities. One tune he liked to play was Judy Collins's 1967 hit song "Clouds" (a.k.a. "Both Sides Now" written by Joni Mitchell), in open G-tuning. It was, in Bill's opinion, a perfect way to close out the *Circle* record, and Randy did it in one take.

With the words of a song from our age in your head as he plays, it somehow captures the essence of all the music we had done in those great six great days. We had looked at both sides then, and they both looked wonderful.

Break time

Playback with Doc and Maybelle

It was happening! We were in the studio with Earl, Doc, Maybelle, Randy Scruggs, Jeff, Ibby, and Les. And in this photo is Bill, the Producer! (also the band's manager at this time). I picked up Bill's camera that was always laying around, and shot this moment as we listened back to Maybelle's "Keep on the Sunny Side." Dino, barely visible in the foreground, told me later this moment would forever be etched in his memory as one of the best of all the records he had made, and that was many.

It would be a few years until I asked Marty Stuart (who was about twelve when *Circle* was recorded) to drive me to Maybelle's house to give her a gold record for *Will the Circle Be Unbroken*—with her name on it. He knew the way, and I was too nervous to drive. I was going to visit Mother Maybelle Carter! It was a nice house a bit outside Nashville, and we pulled in and sat there in the driveway a few moments—had to get my nerve up.

She was cordial, answering my knock at her door, and invited us to come in. After greetings, she asked, "How are you and the rest of the Dirty Boys doin'? Been a while since I have seen you." Maybelle always called us "the dirty boys," which was fine with me.

Listening in the control room L–R standing: Randy Scruggs, Ibby, Earl, Bill McEuen, Jeff. Seated: Doc, Maybelle, Dino Lappas

Maybelle Carter and the boys

I had played a festival earlier in the year with her in West Virginia and sat in her limo for a couple of hours, listening to the Grand Ole Opry tape with the "girls" wailing in the background out of tune and laughing about stuff. She asked then about the Dirty Boys then, too, and it cracked me up.

She was very happy about her gold record (with her name on it!) but happier just to be alive, around, smiling, and chatting. She said, "I didn't even know that many people even heard these old songs. . . . You boys want some lemonade?" She set down the gold record and poured some lemonade she had just made into frosted glasses. Marty later assured me that she meant it about the songs and did not realize the deep impact she made with her voice and guitar style.

Marty and I were next to her music room, right off the front entrance, where people would gather Friday or Saturday nights and pick. Some would drift in from the Opry after they played, and some just came to pick. She welcomed them all.

Mother Maybelle was the nicest person I think I have ever met. When we were recording one of her songs, the phone rang in the control room. I answered it. The conversation went kind of like this:

Caller: "Hi! This is the attorney for Columbia Records legal department. I understand you are recording Maybelle Carter today. I wanted to let you know we have given the OK to record one song with her. Thank you. Good luck with it." I thanked him, told him we were getting close to recording with her, and I would tell the producer . . . and hung up.

Bill asked me who the call was. I said "Nobody important. Just a question." When the call came in, we were recording the fourth song with Maybelle and had one more to go. We knew this was important recording and continued. I told Bill later that day. He agreed with my comment about the lawyer.

Vassar and His Fiddle

Don't assume, because you are often wrong without all the facts. On NGDB's second trip to Japan, three years after recording *Circle*, Vassar came along to "spice up the show." Jethro Tull was on tour there also, and as Ian Anderson had the night off and was hanging out in the lobby, I invited him to our Tokyo concert. At dinner at the hotel after show, Anderson described Vassar to his bandmates as "someone who looked like a Georgia cop that played the fiddle."

Their road manager said he was responsible for the famous backstage rider requirement of "sorted by color, with no brown M&Ms" line in their rider. He had a reason, for if he did not find brown M&Ms he knew the rest of their eighty-page rider was all addressed. If they were not sorted? He checked everything. I was glad then that NGDB rider was much simpler.

Having known Vassar only a couple of weeks, we had no idea what he was thinking about as we waited between songs. After knowing him and playing with him, it was apparent his thoughts were about something other than music and that the music that came out of his fiddle was of the moment and as much of a surprise to him as it was to us. He had certain licks, yes, that he liked to put into a tune, but much of his playing was from the heart and soul of the fiddle, and his constant struggle was trying to "get that dad bime fiddle to mind." Sometimes he even said, "I can't get it to do what I wanted," and sometimes it would be "now listen to that fiddle! How did it do that? Dad bime!"

Vassar Clements

Jimmy Martin and Vassar Clements

The two giants (in our minds) of music, playing together, shows the love Jimmy Martin had for Vassar's notes. With just a little playing between takes, the conversation was hilarious (found on the remaster of *Circle* CD put out in 2002). The self-proclaimed King of Bluegrass lived up to the hype and, in my experience, was not the type of person who would tell a lie for any amount of money. Hype? Now that's different!

Vassar knew of Jimmy's contributions to Bill Monroe's music, which they were discussing here. Jimmy says he wrote the bridge to Monroe's famous song "Uncle Pen" and other contributions for which he did not get credit. They laugh about things not learned as youths, but they continued to put out great music. This chatter is on the remastered CD (2002), but I couldn't get it on the LP version I did around 2011.

Jeff became great friends with Jimmy . . . about twenty-five years later. Jeff made him laugh. I was jealous and happy for him at the same time! There is something about knowing the other

Jimmy and Vassar

person has also spent years on a bus, going around looking for those who will listen to you. That was a bond that Jimmy did not know about at first, but it was one that counts. It is hard to figure out, as I write this, why some people chose to do it at all—go from town to town, looking for a crowd to play to, being away from home, driving 1,500 miles to get a check, playing your music for forty-five to seventy-five minutes, so you can. . . . Well, it's something to do!

I feel lucky to get to do it and grateful there are people out there to listen.

"You Are My Flower" Session

As we cut "You Are My Flower," it felt like such a lot of instruments, but there were only six. The one that can barely be seen is Fadden on autoharp, adding such important tones that if you took his strums out, it would be missing something authentic. His restraint was perfect, as licks were coming from Dobro and guitar a lot. Vassar stepped out on this tune, and I later realized that was good to change it around a bit.

L–R: John McEuen, Norman Blake, Randy Scruggs. Junior Huskey (back middle), Earl Scruggs

Vassar Gets It

Darn him! Look at the neck, Vassar! Bill caught Vassar in one of those moments of loving what he was doing, playing the fiddle like none other. The space his music came from was occupied by the many forms he loved, and over the years after *Circle*, his investigations into other fields were extraordinarily broad, and he conquered all.

Never uttering a bad word about anyone that I recall, nor using foul language other than "dad bime," you would never know he played the fiddle if you just met him. Clements would ask who you were, where you lived, what you did, and things of that nature. He would be interested in all of it, but not bring up the fiddle unless you did.

I had seen him backstage at festivals (well after *Circle*), people chatting away, asking him questions and such. He would often hand his fiddle, the special one he got from John Hartford with the carved god's head, to someone, saying "can you hang on to my fiddle? . . . I have to go get a cup of coffee. I'll be right back." He sometimes didn't come back for fifteen to thirty minutes, as other people would talk to him along the way. When he returned, he would retrieve his fiddle from the nervous person keeping an eye on it for him, relieving them from fiddle watch duty.

Vassar did have a strong dislike for cheese, something we found out at the *Circle* sessions at lunch one day. Some of us were ordering cheese sandwiches. I asked Vassar if he wanted one, "Ain't nothin' but rotten milk!" he answered and turned it down. Years later at a gig I sometimes would bring him a cheese sandwich as a joke and would end up eating it myself.

Vassar gets it

Vassar's Vision

I went on for years wondering where Vassar got his notes. It seemed like they were out there in space, somewhere only he could get to collect them. The strangest thing about it all was he rarely looked at the neck or strings but looked around the room and other places.

Vassar's vision

Jimmy Martin's Opinions

Jimmy Martin was a person who thought everyone had a right to his opinion. He often bragged about his tombstone in the graveyard, one with an inscription on it that says, "Here lies the King of Bluegrass." The funny thing about this bragging was that it was true. His rhythm guitar and singing were "impickable." He also knew how to choose songs that "said" his attitude, like , "Losin' You (Might Be the Best Thing Yet)."

In the key of F, I was nervous about holding up the banjo part that I had learned from recordings of J. D. Crowe when he picked with Martin. J. D. was his best banjo player, and I could not come up to his mark, especially with the banjo that I had. The good banjo that sounded much better than the one I played on *Circle* was stolen in Miami, three weeks before the sessions. I bought the *Circle* banjo in Gainesville, Florida, on the way to Nashville with the band after the show there. Martin made me play so hard during "Walkin' Shoes" that my banjo bridge broke . . . it was good practice! My Circle banjo now resides in Cleveland's Rock and Roll Hall of Fame.

I look at this photo, and I am taken back to that time of recording with the King of Bluegrass, and loved holding down the banjo spot for him. Les, Ibby, and Jeff sang great on the songs, and it did not sound like folk music.

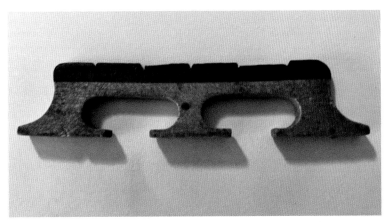

My banjo bridge that broke during the recording of "Walkin' Shoes"
PHOTO BY JOHN McEUEN

I remember calling Jimmy twenty-five years later to talk about what he wanted me to say as I inducted him into the International Bluegrass Music Association, something Orin Friesen and I pushed for a couple of years. Martin wanted me to make sure that people knew he "told it like it was or is." Giving me an example, he said, "like this new song I just wrote for my new ex-wife, called 'I Shouldn't Have Said I Do, But I Did.'" That was Jimmy, short and to the point. The way the King of Bluegrass would want it done.

I played better banjo with Jimmy than I could by myself. His rhythm was perfect, driving you with him, and his voice drove to hit the notes where they needed to be. It was like playing pool: One plays better when you are playing with people better than you.

Jimmy Martin's D Position Capo

Jimmy Martin's prized D-28 Martin guitar would, like Doc's Gallagher guitar, "ring like a bell," in his hands. It had high "action" and was meant for rhythm, at which Jimmy was the best. The fingerboard inlay of his name matched his effervescent personality and somehow made you realize you needed to listen to him.

Martin's way of picking has been emulated by many. For his licks (he would put them either at an intro or between verses), he would hold the flat pick down on a string just before playing the note, pushing hard, then fire it off and then the pick would go to the next string and lay on it before it was picked. It happened quick and made the notes (usually always the lower strings) jump out. If you just picked the notes, like so many of us would, they would not have the same impact as "Martin style" would. I don't think he ever gets credit for that.

I don't know of Jimmy ever doing much lead on the first, second, or third strings because he left the high notes to the other instruments. Those low-string lead licks, though, stood out and often set the mood for the song. We all learned a lot from Jimmy about how to play bluegrass right.

Jimmy Martin's guitar

"Grand Ole Opry Song" with Jimmy Martin

Doing the "Grand Ole Opry Song" with Jimmy Martin was extreme fun; as his guitar was blaring in my headphones, I played. Vassar is not visible, but he was there, sitting on the other side of Martin.

It is amazing that these five instruments can make so much music, and it all starts with the great rhythm of Jimmy's guitar and then his vocals, then Jeff, Ibby, and Les come in on the choruses and round it out. When he sang "about a gang of fellers from down at Nashville" it felt good to be in that gang.

Jimmy liked the 5-string picking all the time (my kind of guy!), and Les, who always had good rhythm, kept the rhythm tight with mandolin chops. When he put his song into the lyric, "we'll sing 'The Sunny Side of the Mountain,'" it was cool and, although not the original lyric, fit great. That was a surprise to us! Jimmy was full of energy that he brought to his music, an energy that was difficult for some to take but great to be around.

"My Walkin' Shoes

Jimmy and the boys

One time (around 1978) I was playing a festival in West Virginia (solo), and I went to watch his set. Although I was careful, as I did not want him to see me, he started yelling from stage, "I see John McEuen out there! If he isn't too good, were gonna have him come up here and pick with us, in fact, I'm just gonna wait rite here until he gets up here with his banjer." My banjo was in the rental car, about fifty yards away. I ran and got it, tuned up, and picked a couple songs with him. I don't know what they were; they went by so fast. It was pure fun, I remember that.

Jimmy Martin, "My Walkin' Shoes"

Here we were in a dream element of being in a real bluegrass band, and Les and I were ready. Vassar was hot as always. Junior always on the money, and the guys sang it like real "grassers." Although Jeff asked me a month before the sessions "who is Jimmy Martin?," he was familiar with his music and just did not know it because Bill and I played some of his songs in those early years when we performed as the Fall River Tar Heels. But Jeff did not have any Jimmy Martin albums; I had every one of them from those earlier years. Jeff was into more of the folk music and songwriter songs. We all tried to be aware of what was happening, but he was a real aficionado of Ian and Sylvia, Hoyt Axton, and the Greenbrier Boys, and some songwriters around us in the SoCal music scene of the time. Jeff liked songs that were deeper or told a story more, and some of the bluegrass songs were, well, just different types of stories.

Here we are in the midst of a run-through of Martin doing "Walkin' Shoes," and it is all in full swing. Fadden plays a part with Vassar's fiddle that sounds perfect—crazy, notes everywhere, and the zaniness of bluegrass in full tilt. My banjo worked well for "Shoes," capoed at the fifth fret.

I was envious of Jeff and his later-in-life relationship with Jimmy because they became good friends over the years. During Martin's yearlong battle with cancer, which took him from us, Jeff went to see him several times in hospice. I don't sing that much, but Jimmy liked (as Martin called him) "little Jeff's" singing, and they got along great. Jeff, Ibby, Les, and I were all fortunate to have Jimmy Martin in our recordings with this album, and his later friendship that brought us a lot of great music and laughs.

Jimmy and the Boys

When Jimmy worked on vocals with you, he would not stop until you got it right. Gary Scruggs here on the right side of photo was working with Ibby, Jeff, and Les. I sat listening while they got it together, musing on Martin's little ponytail, the greatest bluegrass ponytail at the time! Gary Scruggs was instrumental in part of this running smoothly, the perfect bridge (as Earl's oldest son) as he "represented" Earl and was respected as a musician.

Gary would go on to produce and play with Waylon Jennings for several years (after the Earl Scruggs Revue "retired"), write some beautiful songs (of which NGDB did two of them—"Speed of Life" and "Lowlands"), but here he had all that in front of him, yet to do.

Jimmy Instructs Les

Not sure what Les was trying to sort out with Jimmy, but this shot always amused me, as Les looks older than Martin! It was probably the phrasing of "stay on your side of town, honey I won't be around" or something of that nature in "My Walkin' Shoes," the song we are doing here. Jimmy's southern drawl was kind of hard to understand at times, and we were still worried about "doing right" and being up to his mark. But once the music got going everything was fine.

Bill and I used to play this song, and it was one we wanted to record for sure with Martin. I think the other guys did better on it than I did, but overall we were happy with the outcome. It was one take, and that was it!

L–R: John McEuen, Jimmie Fadden, Jimmy Martin, Les Thompson, Jeff Hanna (back turned)

"Losin' You (Might Be the Best Thing Yet)"

Recording some of these without headphones was a good thing for cutting this type of music, as we had to listen to each other, the room, and what was in it. What was in it here was Martin's loud

L–R: Les Thompson, Jimmy Ibbotson, Jeff Hanna, Jimmy Martin, John McEuen

D-28 Martin guitar (he played hard!), other instruments, and the vocals. Backing up Jimmy Martin vocally was a feat not many could accomplish back then, but Les, Jeff, and Ibby handled it. It was good we had that rehearsal day with him, which made it go smoother in the studio.

This shows the restraint the others had, which should be called "taste," to not add washboard or guitars that weren't needed to this cut. They got to sing! And sing they did, sounding like they came from Kentucky and the grass of blue.

Fadden and Vassar did a double solo, as I tried to keep coming up with all the J. D. Crowe licks I could muster, which is what Martin liked. He would say "Get that banjer right in my ear!"

I found out on this trip that "banjer" is actually an approved pronunciation of the instrument! Earl and others called it that. Doc would use "banja" when he mentioned it, as in "Way Downtown."

Vassar's Magic

Vassar playing was not a very "telling" thing; that is, you could not learn much by watching him unless you listened quick and close. His fingers barely moved! His bow was art in motion and did not give a lot away as to what he was doing. The sound that came out of his fiddle, though, was astonishing. Never a mistake (OK, maybe once in a week), maybe one time through would be better than another, but it was always good.

I was doing a film score session about eighteen years later with him, and I went out to the studio to pass out the chord charts for the tune we were going to cut. Five other Nashville cats—players— were in the studio, and they needed to sound like they knew the song! Vassar looked at the chart sitting on his music stand, tilted his head to the right, and looked at it . . . then head to the left, then took the chart and turned it upside down on the music stand. "There . . . that's better!" and everyone laughed. No one laughed when he played.

Vassar Clement

Vassar Clements

I thought that was his way of maybe saying "I don't need a chart," or "I can't read a chart while I play," or something. He didn't need it and he could not read it, but he was a Nashville cat for sure. He would listen and learn where the song was going, and when a solo for him came up, he was ready.

Remembering during that session, I had him come into the control room to listen back. He had just played an incredible lick on a part of the tune, and I wanted to see how it was done. He stood there listening, holding his pipe and fiddle, and said when he heard it "Dad Bime! I don't reckon how anyone could do that!" He tried twice, gave up, and we went on to the next tune.

Vassar Clements Bears Down

This is Vassar getting serious, concentrating on listening to what was coming out of his fiddle. After he played a hot solo, it was not uncommon for him to laugh about "what that fiddle can do!" Vassar looks at his fiddle this time, something he rarely did. He usually played with his eyes shut or looking around space in the room. We were still new to his ways and, thanks to those few days of rehearsal at Earl's house, realized what a giant of a player he was in such a humble frame.

As we ran down "Orange Blossom Special" one time (with Ellis Padgett subbing for Junior on this one)—well, we "rehearsed it" halfway through—we were ready to start the iconic song of bluegrass fiddlers, with Vassar playing some licks that others emulated often over the years.

Ervin Rouse is credited as writer, publishing the song in 1938, and recorded it first in 1939. It became a staple of the bluegrass world, one that would allow the fiddler to improvise during the long E jam section. After Ervin had toured the train, the Orange Blossom, as it was in Jacksonville, Florida, he went home and wrote the instrumental to pay homage to the train (the words he added later). Every fiddler would put in his best licks during that buildup in E, up until the bridge, which always drove people crazy. We loved what Vassar did with it, building up to the bridge, and the way he played this classic was . . . classic!

"OBS," as bluegrassers call it, has been recorded countless times over the years—Johnny Cash (with two harmonicas he played on stage), Bill Monroe, Chet Atkins and the Boston Pops, and many other bluegrass bands. But the one that shows the power of an instrumental in bridging borders comes from Electric Light Orchestra, one of the many groups that recorded this song, in 1974. I always like to think they might have heard this *Circle* version.

Vassar Clements

Vassar Clements

Vassar on "Avalanche"

In action, Vassar played with precise notes. Even if slightly out of tune you would not notice, he would adjust automatically. I remember after playing one song he said, "This dad bime thing's outta tune," but you would not have known anything was amiss.

He is bearing down here as we run thru "Avalanche" before recording it, with the whole band playing on this take off of "Paddy on the Turnpike." Ibby's guitar solo surprised even him!

I think it was the fleeting moment of being "onstage live" that got him through it. Jeff's washboard Vassar liked, and his time was perfect, something he would exhibit often on *Circle*.

I made a mistake at the 2:13 mark that I am embarrassed about to this day! I knew we couldn't cut it over and all the rest as good as it was and decided to wait and see if someone commented on it. So far, no comment!

After using "Paddy" to set up the tune, Clements takes us to some far-out spaces where only he would go in where he let us hear the future of fiddle music. With licks using "long bow" techniques in the back half of the song, getting as many notes out of a bow draw as possible, Vassar plows down this mountain pass in the front of a skier outrunning the "Avalanche." Well after *Circle* came out, we have heard other fiddlers play some of the licks from this tune in other songs, showing his impact on the fiddle world. Vassar, he came, he "sawed," and he conquered.

Vassar Looks up at "Hillbilly Heaven"

That Vassar could play such incredible notes while gazing around the room, not watching what he was doing, was a testament to his playing. He could play it sweet or hot or backup, all without looking. Somehow, he had that magic in him in a way I had only seen once before, in Scotty Stoneman when twenty-year-old me played with Scotty at the Ash Grove in Hollywood. I was so thankful that Vassar had corralled his alcohol demons so he could be with us a lot longer than Scotty. Vassar was in total control of his instrument, listening himself to his fiddle, and what it was doing.

Vassar Clements

Sometimes he would say, "Dad bime! Did you hear what that fiddle did there?" I would follow by asking him to play that for me, what he had just done, to which his answer was: "Dad bime. I don't reckon how I did that." He would try unsuccessfully to replicate some great lick he had just recorded and not quite get it!

When he picked the guitar on "Honky Tonkin," it seemed like the same thing—just play around the song, free form, whatever came up, his guitar noodling made sense! We would try to figure out that great guitar solo of his over the next couple of years but gave up. It was early "Hillbilly Jazz," Vassar's style that he created a few years later and for which he became known.

Vassar didn't "know" music, he knew sounds. He couldn't—or more likely didn't need to—read nor follow a chart for songs, nor could he read music. He would listen to the song and find a place.

But he could find any note on the fiddle that you might throw at him and make it tweet like a bird. Clements's "Listen to the Mockingbird" on the album we did after *Circle*, called *Stars and Stripes Forever*, we captured his "trick" best. He does a bunch of birdcalls in this fiddle contest song (with the fiddle!), and you would swear there are birds there.

We took Vassar to Japan on our second tour there for a month in the mid-1970s, where he had his own worshippers ogling his notes. His notes had gone ahead of us and were spreading the word: "Mr. Clements is in town!"

Vassar, "Dad bime!"

Young Vassar Clements came from Florida, sawing his way from Kissimmee to the top of bluegrass mountain, along the way taking jazz, swing, Hank Williams, and rock and roll into his hands, and surviving quite eloquently note-wise. Unknown to us when we met him, he had played on countless bluegrass artists' records, been in a few bands, and with dozens of groups at concerts and such over the years, leading up to the *Circle* recording. Along the way, the music business part of it was not always easy for him. His talent was so immense, it surprised me that he had done so many other things while still having that incredible talent, yet remained unknown to those outside the bluegrass field. We also did not know that he had recently battled alcohol—and won.

Around 1949, the twenty-one-year-old Clements traveled by bus to ask to audition for Bill Monroe but was told he would have to return the next day. Clements was crestfallen, lacking the money for either a hotel room or return bus trip. Monroe gave him money for a night's lodging, and the next day Clements auditioned and was hired! He remained with Monroe for seven years, recording with the band, but I never knew that. Credits were only for the "star" of an album, Bill Monroe! (Vassar had been that mysterious fiddler who played the lightning-fast "Tall Timber" on a Monroe album, a song I redid with him and the other hot fiddler on it, Bobby Hicks, on *String Wizards* more than forty years later). Vassar soon became one of the most distinctive, inventive, and popular fiddlers in bluegrass music. His virtuosity and ability to blend several different genres, including swing and hot jazz, occasionally mixing it with bluegrass, made him a much-sought-after session musician.

Between 1957 and 1962, he was a member of Jim and Jesse and the Virginia Boys. Vassar also recorded and played with Jimmy Martin, but again no credit was given. He gained recognition "within the trade" of bluegrass, joining Flatt & Scruggs on the popular theme to the hit television sitcom *The Beverly Hillbillies.* Stardom was within his grasp.

I would find out, getting to know him after the *Circle* album, by the mid-1960s his struggles with alcohol had left him making a living in strange jobs: the Kennedy Space Center in Florida as a plumber; a Georgia paper mill; and a switchman for Atlantic Coast Line Railroad. Vassar even sold insurance. The one he would talk to me about the most driving between jobs I hired him to be with me on—with pride—was when he once owned a potato chip franchise in Huntsville, Alabama (Charles Chips). Vassar drove a potato chip truck!

Sobering up, he told his dying mother he would never touch alcohol again. Returning to Nashville in 1967, he became a much-sought-after studio musician. Four years after, I would meet him, thanks to Earl. He had said he would not touch alcohol again to his mother, and there was plenty of it around. After all, we were musicians. But he never did.

This shot, Bill caught Vassar in the heat of battle doing what he did best during a run-through on a song. It was amazing to me that during a run-through on a song in the key of A, we had stopped a moment to discuss arrangement. Vassar plucked his strings during this pause, and the A string was a few cents flat. No one had noticed it was flat while he played, as he was automatically or subconsciously adjusted his fingers to make it in tune. He said, "Dad bime . . . this thing is outta tune." He tuned it up, and we continued.

Besides the constant surprise of a waterfall of notes coming out of his fiddle, I had never heard "dad bime" before, either. Those were his worst words, "swear words," I ever heard him say. And he used them all the time!

In 1974 I asked him if he wanted to go to Japan with NGDB. The *Circle* album was big there, and he could be a "star," which he was to the Japanese. We spent a week in the Tokyo Hilton, playing outlying concert halls, and then about fourteen more shows all over Japan.

Between the Tokyo shows, while waiting for the next one, various guys would wander around the shopping areas close to the hotel. I didn't know Vassar had been admiring a watch at a jewelry store. Finding out when he asked me to go with him to see "something" a couple of blocks away, he pointed at it and said, "Look at that dad bime watch! Finest timepiece ever made, that Seiko watch!" He didn't buy it. I got the band guys to put up the money, and we bought it for him and gave it to him the next day. He was astonished and said, "Dad bime! Thanks!"

Vassar was a man of few words and a whole lotta notes. He thought fast. I asked him a few days later how that watch was doing for him. In a flash, with a smile, he said "Western Union called me this mornin' t'see what time it was!" I said "Dad bime!"

Dad bime, Vassar, you sure were good! Thanks for being with us.

The Great Roy Acuff

"He's coming," Roy Acuff that is, we heard from someone. We still were not absolutely sure if he was going to record with us. He was in the parking lot and coming into the studio to meet and, possibly, record with us. We still were not certain if he was going to record, especially after entering the studio and standing there, skeptically looking around the room. He had celebrity eyesight, you know, the kind that looks around the room and never looks right at you. Roy was being cautious. After all, he was co-owner of the biggest publishing house in Nashville (Acuff-Rose), the Grand Ole Opry's King of Country Music, and did not have to be there.

But ever the businessman, Roy knew these sessions would be good for him, and—for business. We were a "pop" group to him because we were on "the Devil's rock-and-roll charts," and he needed to spread the Acuff word to some new ears. We also were planning on doing some of his songs (and a couple he published), him singing, and getting him more notoriety (and publishing income) than he imagined.

Please don't get me wrong. Roy was nice. After the *Circle* in 1988, he let me talk him into introducing Gary Hart (who was running for president) to the Opry audience. That photo of the two of them shaking hands was in eighty-eight newspapers! A week later, Hart spent too much time on a boat and dropped out of the race.

Charlie Collins, his rhythm guitarist for years, told me something like "Roy and I were driving back to Nashville after a date he had in St. Louis. It was the week before your session for *Circle*

Roy Acuff and Earl

Roy Acuff

were to start. He said 'I don't know . . . I met these boys . . . these young men . . . or old men, I don't know. Their faces were all covered in hair. I don't know what I'm a gettin' in to.'

By the time we got to recording with Roy, first up was one of his signature songs, "Wreck on the Highway." We were somewhat "comfortable" with our position. That is to say, we had settled in. It was day six in "our" studio, we were doing a special project, and all the band knew it. This song had most of the things I loved hearing about in country/bluegrass music: a wreck, alcohol and its evils, death, cars, and praying—except "nobody prayed."

Having met him the previous week, when Earl took us for Roy's lecture in his office on music, about "recording on Monday, performing the next few days on the road, then weekends at the Opry, playing on the road after the Opry shows, going from town to town on Sunday thru Thursday to get back for the Friday and Saturday Opry shows." Well, he sounded like, in Earl's grudgingly expressed words, telling us as he was driving some of us to our hotel, "That s.o.b. (Acuff) . . . he sounds like he invented country music!"

I saw Acuff's lecture as the commercial side of the music trying to show power over bluegrass. It didn't work with Earl. Scruggs was humbly confident of his position in music.

We weren't sure Roy was going to come on recording day, though. Bill had saved him for Friday, just in case, and by that time *The Tennessean* (the Nashville newspaper) had published an interview with Roy where he said "those Nitty Gritty boys . . . well . . . I don't know if they're young boys or old men . . . or what . . . they're all covered with hair!" Which we were.

Roy balancing his fiddle bow

But, on Friday he showed! We were ready for him, but he didn't know until that first recording that it would be OK for him. He came back into the studio after playback in the control room and did one of his "signature licks" from his Opry shows—and balanced the fiddle bow on his nose. We were "in," after this arduous week and accepted as a group of pickers who would honor his sound.

We moved on, a little less tenuously, to the next song, "Precious Jewel," a tender little ballad with Oswald's Dobro crying all the way through.

Jeff and Roy

Being "inspected" by the King of Country Music, Jeff was quiet and nervously mindful of his position. He was getting ready to cut a song with Roy Acuff as the unknown guitar player in some band of youngsters from the West Coast. Les, at his position next to Vassar, was preparing his licks. But Roy accepted us, and he was there to record. It was up to us to do the rest.

Vassar's lead-in to his solo is spectacular, as is his solo, and Fadden laid back just right. It was Oswald's Dobro, Acuff's "sound," though, that made this recording come to life. Crying out after the lyric, his answers to the vocal were right in the pocket.

Roy Acuff and Jeff Hanna

An hour before the first recording started, Oswald had his Dobro all unstrung and was putting on "new wires" (as he called them). He went by string numbers and put the first through the sixth string on and then went to tuning it. He asked for the third string on the guitar to pick a note, so he could tune his third string to it. He didn't know it was a G note, but he got it right, and tuned the rest to it. It amazed me that "Bashful Brother" Oswald did not know the names of his strings on his instrument! He did know the number.

Oswald played from his heart, with more soul than anyone in the room, making that Dobro cry with anguish depending on what the singer was feeling.

Acuff felt good about the cut and went in to listen to it, again giving his approval . . . much to our relief! We still had "Circle" to do (doing it last) and were three songs away from recording it. It looked like he was going to hang in until the final song.

Roy Checks out the Control Room

Roy Acuff was serious about his music, as his often-serious face would let anyone know. His music was "easy" to play, but there is a good way and a bad way to play "easy music." We were happy that our version of easy was good enough to pass the Acuff test, as in this photo he seems to be looking for approval for his singing first . . . the music, he was comfortable with, more so with each song cut as we went on.

Roy Acuff

We were actually making a record with Roy Acuff—something that did not hit me at the time. We were just trying to hold our own in his world, worried about it at first. But by day two (three days pre-Roy), we'd found out the artists were such fans of each other, they seemed as if they were on vacation. It did solve one question I had: I wondered what had driven them here. I know Earl had a lot to do with getting many involved, but he could not swing getting Josh Graves on Dobro nor Bill Monroe.

When we heard things from Maybelle, Travis, Doc, and Earl, talking to each other, like: "why haven't we recorded together before?" "Really glad to be doing this with you!" "Finally, in the studio together." It became apparent that we were along for the ride. And, what a ride it was turning out to be on this the last day for recording.

Acuff didn't wear headphones, but some NGDB did. I always like hearing Jeff's right-on rhythm guitar, and I like to hear it as the pick hits the strings. And the lead vocal is good to have in one ear to find a lick that goes with a lyric. But this was a different situation, and sometimes it was good just to listen to the room as that was going to be the record!

Setting up "I Saw the Light" and "Circle"

It was time to stuff people into the studio for "I Saw the Light" and "Will the Circle Be Unbroken," which was a "gleeful" job, a fun thing, good songs . . . and special moments that didn't last long enough.

And it all came together as it is on this album, the record of the event. There are some people here I didn't know, most of them I did, and they all sang this music of historical importance. Since

The album's title did not come about until all the songs had been recorded, with the last one being "Will the Circle Be Unbroken." For many years we thought it was strictly a Carter Family song, as that is where we—and the general public—first heard it. At the time of this recording, it was commonly attributed to A. P. Carter and the Carter Family, even though their original 1938 recording of it is known as "Can the Circle Be Unbroken," which was unknown to us at the time.

It is known now that A.P. took a song of old, called "Will the Circle Be Unbroken," written in 1907 by Charles Gabriel and Ada Habershon, and reworked it to make a "new" song of it.

Bill had the albums' recorded tapes, and in sequencing the songs, it became obvious to him that "Circle" was to be the title of the record. Not sure about it before recording, but as soon as it was done, he, and we, were sure. This "new" album of old music recorded new was to be, what else, but *Will the Circle Be Unbroken*.

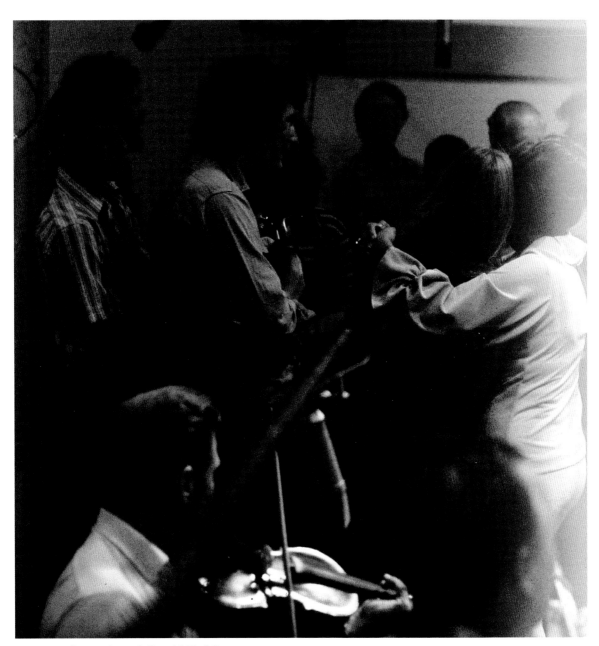

Setting up "I Saw the Light" and "Circle"

things happened fast, there was no time to change shirts! Sometimes, you can figure out who is in the photo by checking what shirt they had on when you saw their face. In this case, Jeff is just the other side of Randy Scruggs. I believe that is Chet Flippo in the background in this shot, the famous writer from *Rolling Stone* who helped get the word out on this album; he appears in one other shot, too. Thanks, Chet!

Passing the Acuff "Test"

Here we are, taking our "Acuff test," as he listened to the first cut we did together . . . just like this. We didn't know if he was happy or not because his poker face didn't have a lot of "tells" in it. He was concerned and had a lot to keep in mind in doing this unusual project. What if we had sounded like crap, to put it bluntly, and put the King of Country Music in a difficult position? Would he finish the album?

After this playback, and we had to do it twice, the playback, is when he went out to the studio balancing the fiddle bow on his nose, indicating in his way that it sounded good and he was happy. He was staying on for the rest of the session. (Part of Roy's "stage act" would be things like yo-yos, balancing the fiddle or its bow on his nose, and walking around the stage and then playing it.)

Roy Acuff

Man with Voice

We were ready to cut the first song with Roy Acuff, "Wreck on the Highway." The ever-pensive Acuff showing signs of worry about working with a bunch of "hippies." As it was Friday, and he was the last artist to record before doing the last song "Will the Circle Be Unbroken," we were a little bit anxious ourselves about what we were going to do behind him. We were also somewhat confident, as the week had been incredible, and everything was going smoothly.

But this was Acuff, who was dubbed by the Opry as the King of Country Music!

We rehearsed "Wreck" a bit—once, that is! He listened to us and kind of sang. Then Dino had all the mics set, and he went into the control room to mark the board. (This is putting down people's names on the various mic channels on the mixing board, their EQs, and things of that nature.)

Acuff was ready, but there was one more thing. He felt compelled to tell us "his philosophy of recording" before we started cutting: "Now, I'll tell you all a little secret of my policy in the studio . . . I find it true . . . and I believe it is true . . . and that is, once you decide to go in and record a number, put everything you got into it. Because . . . don't say 'oh, we'll take it over and do it again' . . . because every time you go through it, you lose just a little something. Especially, a man with voice. So, let's do it the first time and t'hell with the rest of 'em!"

Now we were anxious again, and we cut it! Fadden on harp, Jeff on guitar, and Les on mandolin, all backing up Roy Acuff. The band, along with Oswald, Junior, and Vassar, were sidemen in a dream.

When Roy went into the control room to listen to the playback, we waited in the studio, wondering if we passed muster. Would he approve?

He was HAPPY! We cheered and went to the next song, more confident than the last one.

Oswald Kirby was the basis for Roy's sound, as sometimes guitar players would be for other singers such as Luther Perkins in the Tennessee Three behind Johnny Cash (with the muted strings, which started because he could not play that well at first) or the banjo of Flatt & Scruggs. My mother told me Oswald's crying Dobro always made her cry; I know from that he was integral as part of what became "Roy's sound."

As he would on all the tracks to follow, Roy sang great, giving it his signature sound with Dobro behind his lyrics, and he got it right the first—and only—time.

Last day of recording

Gathering for "Will the Circle Be Unbroken"

Incredible. Confusing? Not really, but exciting for sure. The chatter was immense, with everyone talking to everyone. Jimmy Martin telling Acuff something, studio guy positioning mic stand, and Dino checking something. Junior, as he was always in his position, overseeing quietly from his bass perch. This song was to be what we call an "all skate," where everyone works—just find a place. I grabbed a mandolin (back to camera), and with Martin, Doc, Oswald, Earl, Vassar, Junior (on the right), and the Dirt Band, we had a band!

This moment, frozen in time, is the preparation prior to recording what would become the title of the album. It became obvious to Bill (thinking back to when we finished this old "Carter Family" song) that we had just recorded the title song for the album. Often credited entirely to the Carter Family by others who sang it across the years since the Carters first recorded for Ralph Peer in 1927, "Circle" had become known over the years prior to "song collector" A. P. Carter bringing it to light. He came across both "Can the Circle Be Unbroken" and "Will the Circle Be Unbroken," changing a few words, adding a verse, arranging the song, and making it what it is today.

The feeling in the room was one of ecstasy for me and all the Dirt Band, as we had now done what we came to do: brought these icons together to record with a "pop-rock band of kids" from California who respected all of them. Three different generations making a record, a true record in the sense it was "a record of this event." Being the last song of the last day, it was like a play's last performance. Sad, happy, fun, and calmly intense—I believe everyone knew this would be special to the various audiences out there in record land, as we were getting ready to do it. One could feel it in the room.

Rita Forester (A.P.'s granddaughter, whom I met in 2017) told me A.P. said back then "If this music thing works, I just hope we make enough money so I can buy some restaurant plates," explaining he loved restaurant plates because they would not break. There were a lot of restaurant plates around the house in Hiltons, Virginia; it had worked! My wife Marilyn and I visited Rita a few days in 2017, staying in Maybelle's old house (it was in perfect condition), and we drove to Bristol to see what it might have been like for the Carters in 1927. The road was much better.

Later in the week, when we got home, there in the mail was a gift from Rita: a plate and some of her molasses cookies, with her letter that said, "since you were admiring those plates of A.P.'s, I thought I would send you one . . . the cookies are from an old family recipe." Marilyn cooked up a couple of eggs, put them on the plate, and we sent her a photo with me and the plate of eggs "keeping on the sunny side."

A. F. M. Musician Log

This contract shows the incredible amount of work entailed in doing some of the days. Ten songs in one 15-hour studio day only worked because of so many first takes. Five Jimmy Martin songs, four instrumentals, and "You Are My Flower" all made in that wonderful day. Another aspect is the "studio traffic" because Earl, Junior, and I were the only musicians for "Soldier's Joy," but we were done in about twenty minutes and ready to move on . . . enter Jimmy Martin! Jimmy's "hellos" took up about an hour, as he had a few stories to tell, a joke to make, and all-around camaraderie to make happen.

I look at this now and am amazed with the fact that one of the most important things you can do with your life—if you are a musician—is to record. What takes the least amount of time at one end can lead to great accomplishments at the other. It was just a flash in one sense, one that has had all of us in its light since it happened.

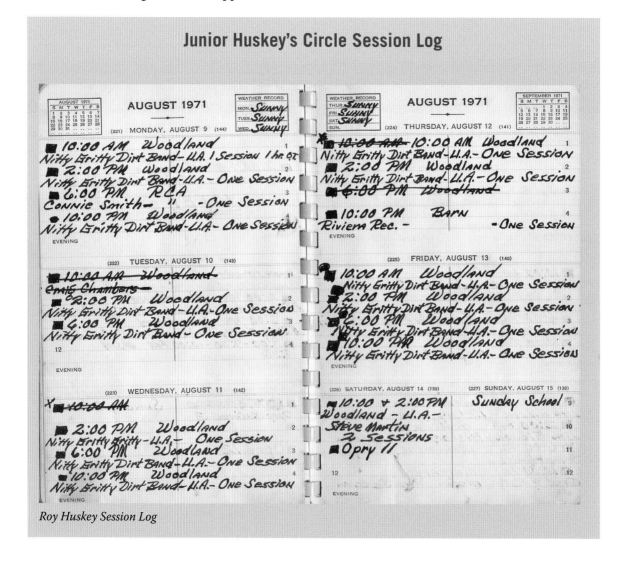

Roy Huskey Session Log

(Employer's name) **United Artists**

Phonograph Recording Contract Blank

AMERICAN FEDERATION OF MUSICIANS
OF THE UNITED STATES AND CANADA

Local Union No. **47**

No. **108546** -R

THIS CONTRACT for the personal services of musicians, made this **25** day of **August** 19 **71** between the undersigned employer (hereinafter called the "employer") and **13** musicians (hereinafter called "employees").

(including the leader)

WITNESSETH, That the employer hires the employees as musicians severally on the terms and conditions below, **and as further specified on reverse side.** The leader represents that the employees already designated have agreed to be bound by said terms and conditions. Each employee yet to be chosen shall be so bound by said terms and conditions upon agreeing to accept his employment. Each employee may enforce this agreement. The leader represents that the employees already designated have agreed to be bound by said terms and conditions. Each employee yet to be chosen shall be so bound by said terms and conditions upon agreeing to accept his employment. Each employee may enforce this agreement. The employees severally agree to render collectively to the employer services as musicians in the orchestra under the leadership of **Walter H. McEuen** as follows:

Name and Address of Studio **Woodland Studios, 1001 Woodland St., Nashville, Tenn.**

Date(s) and Hours of Employment **August 9, 1971 (10a.m. – 1p.m.)(2p.m. – 5p.m.)(6p.m.–9p.m.)**
(10p.m.–1p.m.)

Type of Engagement. **Recording for phonograph records only.**

Plus pension contributions as specified on reverse side hereof.

WAGE AGREED UPON $ **Union Scale**

(Terms and amount)

This wage includes expenses agreed to be reimbursed by the employer in accordance with the attached schedule, or a schedule to be furnished the employer on or before the date of engagement.

To be paid **Within 15 days**

(specify when payments are to be made)

Upon request by the American Federation of Musicians of the United States and Canada (herein called the "Federation") or the local in whose jurisdiction the employees shall perform hereunder, the employer either shall make advance payment hereunder or shall post an appropriate bond.

Employer's name and **United Artists Records**
(Name of Record Company)

Authorized signature

Street address **6920 Sunset Blvd.**

L.A., Calif. **46109141**
City / State / Phone

Leader's name **Walter H. McEuen** Local No. **47**

Leader's signature

Street address **8662 Lookout Mt. Ave.** Phone No.

L.A., Calif.
City / State

Name of Artist or Group **Nitty Gritty Dirt Band**

(1) Label Name **United Artists**

Session No. **2216-B**

Master No.	No. of Minutes	TITLES OF TUNES	Master No.	No. of Minutes	TITLES OF TUNES
	3:35	YOU ARE MY FLOWER		2:47	LOSING YOU
	2:05	SOLDIER'S JOY		2:59	GRAND OLE OPRY SONG
	2:12	FLINT HILL SPECIAL		2:02	WALKIN' SHOES
	3:10	NASHVILLE BLUES		2:23	SUNNY SIDE OF THE MOUNTAIN
	2:34	EARL'S BREAKDOWN		2:45	YOU DON'T KNOW MY MIND

(2) LOCAL UNION NO. & CARD NO.	(3) EMPLOYEE'S NAME (Last, First, Initial) HOME ADDRESS (Street, City, State & Zip)	(4) SOCIAL SECURITY NUMBER (5) MARITAL STATUS & EXEMPTIONS	(6)	PREMIUM RATE	(8) TOTAL SCALE WAGES	(9) CARTAGE	(10) 8% AFM-EPW	(11) H & W
47	McEuen, Walter H.	545-60-7162 M-0	4 sessions		720.00		57.60	1.00
47	Ibbotson, James A.	161-36-7403 M-0	3 sessions		270.00		21.60	1.00
47	Hanna, Jeffrey R.	545-72-3906 M-0	4 sessions		360.00		28.80	1.00
47	Thompson, Leslie S.	556-68-4783 M-0	4 sessions		360.00		28.80	1.00
47	Fadden, Jimmie L.	558-82-9083 M-0	4 sessions		360.00		28.80	1.00
257	Scruggs, Earl E.	240-30-8682 M-0	2 sessions		180.00		14.40	1.00
257	Scruggs, Randy L.	409-78-8111 S-0	2 sessions		180.00		14.40	1.00
257	Taylor, Robert A.	256-28-3453 M-4	1 session		90.00		7.20	1.00
257	Blake, Norman L.	255-62-6089 M-3	1 session		90.00		7.20	1.00
257	Martin, Jimmy	230-30-2079 S-0	2 sessions		180.00		14.40	1.00
257	Padgett, Ellis E.	261-30-2730 M-3	1 session		90.00		7.20	1.00

SEP – 0 1971 ACCOUNTS PAYABLE

FOR FUND USE ONLY:
RECEIVED

(12) Total Pension Contributions (Sum of Column (10)) **11.00**
Make check payable in this amount to "AFM & EPW Fund."

(1) Total Health and Welfare $

Date pay't rec'd_____ Amt. paid_____
Date posted_____ By_____

A. & R. ADMINISTRATOR

4 of 11

Form B-4 Rev. 12-69

Circle musicians log PHOTO BY JOHN McEUEN

Edit Heads

Most important steps were taken by Bill in editing all the tapes together: sequencing the songs, using the constantly running "slow tape" of talking and between-song chatter, and in general, sculpting together a cohesive album from the six days of recording thirty-eight cuts. He called it "his masterpiece" . . . he was right. The Library of Congress inducted it in 2005.

Pictured are the playback/record heads, where the places to cut the tapes were actually located—on the tape. The iron oxide on the opposite side of the tape did its magic, arranging its molecules magnetically to reproduce what it was electronically being fed. Move the tape reels with your hands, back and forth, when you were close to the place to edit, listen carefully, move it back and forth more, and mark the tape with a marker pen, and then the necessary cuts were made with a razor blade slicing the tape. These were to be precise, there was no redo. Bill had recording tape pieces hung around the studio and on various reels, getting them ready to be spliced together for the various sides of the album. It took months!

Bill decided to start this album in a way no one had dared before: with a false start, a mistake! The "Grand Ole Opry Song," with Jimmy Martin singing, was to be the first song, kicked off with banjo, which I messed up on and had to start over. He thought a few seconds of "failibility" would show those listening that we (or in this case, me) were not perfect and catch them off guard. This led to Martin's comment that captures his attitude perfectly: "Earl never did do that!" when I made that mistake on the opening lick and started over. Glad the rest was right!

Bill's sensibilities for this album came from the film world, which he would get in to heavily in later years after USC film school. He wanted to use our paint to apply to his canvas and make the record sound and look great. That he did it is a testament to his abilities and vision. We all thank him for his diligence and choices because he made it to stand the test of time, which it has.

Circle *Tape Editing Heads*

Doug Sax mastering the album

Doug Sax and the Mastering Lab

When recording two-track, you are making the master; it is the tape the "mother" will be made from after mastering to make the "stampers," the discs that actually press the record. Bypassing the mix down from multitrack (sixteen or twenty-four tracks at a time mixing to two-track stereo) to mix live to two tracks and then proceed, a generation is saved; it wasn't a copy of the master multitrack but right from "the source." Each track on a multitrack will bring in some noise, be it ambient room sound, or just air . . . something. With two-track recording, it happens only twice—each track.

Bill wanted the best in the business for mastering, and at the time, this step was to be done by one of the best, Doug Sax. Thanks to Mr. Sax's ears and expertise, this is where we found out "the mistake" that was made when we recorded.

It was with the control room at Woodland Studios where he ran into trouble. The entry door to the control room was next to the left speaker and had a little space; the doorway opened, and it would be right under the left speaker. When the door was shut, there was still a couple of feet of extra space on that side of the control room. This made the bass "fatter," making it so when the mix was being done (and it was done live), the bass in the center was not really in the center. It was off to the right a bit, out of balance but was made up for by the left hallway by the left speaker putting it to center. If noon was center, left was 9:00, right was 3:00, and then the bass was at about 1:30, instead of noon, when the mix was taken to a proper studio too far right.

Doug EQed it (affecting the low and high end of the sound spectrum) and did something else to bring it back to center, saving the day in a way—a way that made it into the industry studio magazine with seven pages about the album mix and its great sound quality. The changes in EQ might not be noticed by everyone, especially in today's earbud and iPhone listening world, but it does make a difference.

This was an unusual album to have Doug master, because bluegrass was not considered real music by most of Hollywood at the time. But it was sound waves, and he knew what to do with the sound waves to best represent them.

Hollywood would learn that this old-timey, Appalachian hillbilly music would go on to be in the Grammy Hall of Fame and the Library of Congress (2005) after becoming a platinum album. This three-record set has now achieved multiplatinum status.

The mastering console only had about eight knobs, but one had to know exactly how to use them, and Doug did. In the foreground you can see Bill's guitar, which he carried often, an old Gibson J-45 that he loved to play blues on, often followed with a Hank Williams song. Also visible is his camera equipment, with which he took all the photos. Bill was a perfectionist, and he often called the *Circle* album "his masterpiece." I agree with that, because if had been left up to me we would have had Doc and Earl, a single album, and a mediocre cover photo in front of a bus!

Mastering the *Circle*

This most important step was watched by Bill and Doug Sax, intently. It was the last chance to get it right in regard to sonic quality or to maybe fix something that could be wrong. A little more top end, little less bass, whatever, but you could not mix it because there are (with any recording at this step) only two tracks. Any changes had to be done with EQ (bass, treble, midrange adjustments), and hope you "got it all." This is where phrases like "inner-diameter distortion," "groove push," and "too loud for last track" would be said.

Definitions: As the groove goes around the record, keep in mind the speed does not change, but the length of the groove does! The outside cut (first one) could be two minutes and make a groove about seventy-five-feet long if you laid out in a straight line. The inside cut (the last one) would have its two minutes in about a fifty-foot-long groove. The outside cuts (cuts away from the middle of the record) are longer and can hold more information more easily than the inside cuts. You cannot put the loudest song on the inside cut; the groove is much shorter, and there is inner-diameter distortion.

Mastering lab

Think of the groove, as it gets to the last cut, how much tighter the turn is than on the outside of the record, where it is almost straight but at the center of the record? The needle leans more heavily on the part of the groove that is on the outside, and well, it tends to create distortion and is good to avoid. The information on the inner diameter can distort if too hot level wise.

Groove push is fairly unavoidable. You who play records or remember playing them, think about how, one turn of the record *before* the music would start, you could hear a little "tinkling" sound—the sound that was coming in less than two seconds, followed by the actual song blaring out. Well, what you hear there is the air from the groove with the information on it activating the needle as it tracks in the empty groove leading up to the song. This sound "effect," or whatever you call it, is always there only buried by the audio level of the music in the groove. Then there is level matching, leveling, limiting or evening out the amount of (audio) level on each track so they match up right with each of the cuts on the album. You do not want the third cut to be a lot hotter, louder, than the first or last cut; they all have to hit the zero line on the dB meters, if done right. This mastering process has to be done with CDs also and is somewhat simpler but still necessary to represent the best of the final product.

If the record is mastered too hot, it is likely the needle will jump out of the groove on the last cut, even if it is the same volume as the first cut. That has to be avoided! So, mastering by a pro is an important step. One tries to get more level on the record's grooves, but you must be careful. *Circle* was cut fairly hot because there were no loud drums, screaming electric guitars, or vocals in the middle of any songs that were loud, fairly even on the audio, and only two tracks with which to deal. It is an amazing, magical, process.

Mastering lab circle one

Cutting the Mustard in Mastering

This great shot would not be discernable unless the previous mastering shots were seen. It shows the process of the actual cutting into the lacquer mother disc during mastering. Visible are the vacuum (to suck up the cut up lacquer, generated by cutting the groove), and the cutting head that would take the signal, the music, from the tape and put it to—actually cutting in to the lacquer— the grooves. Out of a mother disc this process made the stampers, which were cut here.

I remember being told a stamper was good for stamping out about twenty-five thousand discs, then they would be replaced with a new stamper made from the mother disc.

This process all sounds like a space-age fairy tale but goes back a long way. When it is described, you might be inclined to say, "Are you crazy? That won't work!" But it does, and as long as several things are done right, you end up with a "keeper"! And you can't easily copy them!

In LA, there were only a few "mastering engineers," usually ignored (or unknown) by the public, out there digging the music. Thanks to them, we hear it all even and nice on various pieces of playback equipment.

Cutting the mustard mastering

Original tape reel PHOTO BY JOHN McEUEN

Side 4 "Lonesome Fiddle" tape box PHOTO BY JOHN McEUEN

Making the *Circle* Covers

This was the exciting moment the inks were first put on the paper, a process that was much more difficult than it is now. You could tell the *Circle* album was going to be "special," as these printed sheets—"boards"—came out, prior to cutting. They had to be cut, folded, and stacked all precisely prior to getting their records inserted into the printed sleeves, all of which took time . . . a lot of time. In the time it took to make one complete *Circle* album package, you could make about twenty single album covers/jackets and all.

It was the package that kept it from charting! Since the initial run was only twenty-five thousand, they sold out before they got to the stores. The company had to reorder another batch! It would take three weeks to get them—all three records—printed and stamped, and twenty-five thousand covers cut, stacked, filled, and shrink-wrapped to be albums ready to go out the door! The next batch would ship, but preorders would get them snatched up before others could get to them. Another order of twenty-five thousand units, another month, and the same thing. . . .

Billboard would call and ask "How many have you sold this week" to which the answer was none for two to three weeks. They would not chart it! They would call a few weeks later, during a "filling the order to manufacture" period, same thing—none sold. They failed to pick up the fact that twenty-five thousand had sold, instantly, in week 1, week 4, week 9, and so forth.

Finally, about nine months later, the company went to making fifty thousand units at time. This was good, but their first batch of those sold out in a week, and they had to do the same thing, make another fifty thousand. This went on until it became gold (five hundred thousand units), which took a while! Then it reached its first platinum (one million units) level.

Ivy Hill printers

Circle *front cover*

Circle *album layout*

The Cover Laid Out

Here the cover is laid out flat for inspection of colors and registration (making sure the various runs lined up and prep to cut up). It was Bill's great vision that he had to make this album jacket so expensive that one would feel like they had something of value just by holding it, something that would stand up, "stand the test of time," something you wanted to keep. He succeeded in that! I have had people come up to have me sign their *Circle* album, telling me "it's the original," or "got it forty years ago," "I got it when it came out fifty years ago," and they were still in great condition.

Ivy Hill printing

Layin' It Down on Chrome Coat!

A most important step in making the cover was quality control. They are not "just" looking at it, admiring their work; they are judging it, looking for mistakes, improper registration of colors, and general printing of this complicated cover. This was the first run and the first print of this fantastic cover (Grammy nominated!), and it passed inspection. Let the presses roll and get this under way but keep checking the prints along the way. As Woody the Old Indian would say "it's just like downtown! Cut it up like a pie!"

Woody the Old Indian worked for our father and was a mentor to me in many nonmusical ways. His advice was always of value to us, and his words hit home. Bill was making this cover, one major aspect that makes the *Circle* album standout to me, anyway; it seemed like he was saying "this is how good it can get." It is good, Bill. It is your masterpiece, though many things he did grossed more money than this (one measure of success); the *Circle* album would do more than sixty million dollars in sales . . . and it keeps on going.

Layin' it down on chrome coat

Quality control

Time to make the cover for what had become incredible work. Bill loved documenting every step of the way possible, and when he went to Ivy Hill for printing, he insisted on a few things that were unusual, while capturing the essence of what was happening.

One was the choice of paper, chrome coat board, a glossy fourteen-point board that was usually for perfume boxes. He needed enough to cover the six sides of what had become a three-record set (it started as two). Also in his plan were sleeves with various liner notes, photos, printing, and "things that made it look nice."

Three sleeves, the board, and four colors on six surfaces! As the cover was being designed (with help from Dean Torrence, of surf music's Jan and Dean; Dean became a cover designer when Jan had a car wreck and could not perform). Bill saw the necessity for one more chrome coat panel, making that eight surfaces to print on. The record jackets were left to be colorless (black and white), saving some money there; but they were sepia!

All this color Bill determined could not be done right if it was a gang run. In those days, the printing press would run all day, and several different covers might be printed with the same load of inks. This process would make the inks not retain their solid color, like black or deep red, get slightly mixed, or other problems. Covers would possibly "drift" from how they looked from the first to the last one printed. *Circle* had to be uniform. Black had to be black!

Bill wanted it to be consistent. It was, as it was run all by itself on a newly inked press, set just for only the *Circle* album.

This photo shows one of the major steps in that printing, getting the registration and colors right as the album was being printed—quality control. Registration is where you have one set of lines that might be blue, and one set red, then yellow, and they have to *all* line up each time, so photos and lines and such will all line up right. On the first run, Bill watched them as they printed, for an initial run of twenty-five thousand. I know he was anxious to get it together and assemble the first one, and it came out perfect.

When the record company found out this cover was going to cost them about $1.20 each, they said they were "not going to do it!" We had "the power" of *Uncle Charlie & His Dog Teddy* behind us—the previous album that had three radio records on it—and Bill, as producer, boldly threatened "OK. I'll erase the tapes then! I won't need a cover!"

The record companies then could be "yelled at" like that, if you had some hits, which we did thankfully. Thanks to Ibby, Les, Jeff, and Fadden, Bill's production and album cover, we had undisputed success. The companies were more afraid you might leave. A powerful manager or producer could instill fear in the people at a company. Bill was both—manager and producer—and did some of that, instilling "fear," but those in the art and promotion departments liked him. They got along great. Mike Stewart was eventually happy, too!

The First Run Chrome Coat

Finding the right paper was a difficult quest, because the album cover printers had a lot of cheapo stuff they would run albums with, and Bill didn't like the choices. Bill had finally chosen chrome coat board. This cardboard was shiny and firm and held up well. The Ivy Hill Printers (the Hollywood company that printed album covers), knew this was a special project when they saw the board for the covers stacked up, waiting their turn to make the album covers and record jackets.

They ran it by itself as Bill insisted, "Please, no gang print run on this. It needs to be on its own" he told them. A gang run is when more than one project is run in the press, without cleaning the inks, etc. With fresh ink for the *Circle* runs, black was black, red was red, and the tones were all right on the money.

It was exciting to see this come together, and it took most of two weeks to print twenty-five thousand (the initial order, the most the company would do, as the package was so expensive . . . and Mike Stewart thought he would sell ten thousand!). It took another week to cut, stuff the records in the printed sleeves, fold, and shrink-wrap, getting ready to ship. In Bill's words "People will have this album a long time. Better make sure the cover holds up and properly represents all your guys' work. This is a classic!" which it was going to be.

I remastered *Circle* in 2005 for LP (vinyl) and used the same materials; it came out great, the original masters (which I had in my house for twenty-five years) played fine, and Bill's simple comment of "it's perfect!" made my day. This remaster is still available (LP and CD), and while the LP does not include the four extra cuts as the CD remaster does (2002), it has liner notes, and a big poster that is part of the package, along with all the aspects of what made this a special package. I believe it is one that will be around for a while, and "hold up properly." I have often heard from buyers "you know how hard it is to divide a three-record set when you get divorced?!"

First printing of Circle *cover*

A Part of the Circle Passes—Steve and Earl

Bill got this shot right after I introduced Steve Martin to Earl in Nashville 1971. They picked for a while in Steve's room, and Earl was his cordial patient self as he was with everyone. Earl was a nice man who played the fire out of the banjo. Steve was not yet known to country music, and Bill had convinced him to go to Nashville to record, with no target in mind for the recording (it would come out as *The Steve Martin Brothers* album nine years later). Part of Bill's philosophy was to make a record, have it finished, and then take it to see who is interested in taking it.

He used Vassar with Junior and a few other musicians. I even played on a couple of cuts, but the point was, Steve got to meet Earl! Since our teenage years we both had marveled at what Mr. Scruggs could do, and now he was right there in front of him.

Steve had a couple of great tunes he had written by 1971, as he was as serious about his banjo playing as he was with comedy. Part of him wanted to be a banjo picker and was always self-doubting and unsure about his playing. I was fortunate to produce his album *The Crow: New Songs for the Five-String Banjo*, with which we surprisingly won a Grammy for Best Bluegrass Album in 2009. What a strange trip for a couple of Orange County kids.

I will never forget that day in March 2012. Steve called as my wife Marilyn and I walked in New York City's Washington Square, and he simply said, "Did you hear? Earl died." I had not heard that yet, but it was good to come from Steve. They had become friends, too, and Earl loved his picking.

Bye and bye, Earl, bye and bye.

Earl Scruggs and Steve Martin

3

A CIRCLE OF FRIENDS

THE CIRCLE CONTINUES

It is unusual for an album to be so successful for more than fifty years. Since its release in 1972 the *Circle* record—often called by some "The Dark Side of the Banjo" or the father of *O Brother, Where Art Thou?*—has been called by many "the favorite record" in their collection. Remaining a constant seller and continuing to today has been quite a feat, and those who own it treasure it in their collection. The comments in this section are from just a few of those who were involved or around it, all of whom I thank here for their contributions and appreciate the kind comments people have made about the *Circle* album over the years.

Gary Scruggs

Earl's oldest son, Gary, became a friend from rehearsals to sessions and a person I have always looked up to and been amazed by because his own accomplishments are many. He helped us all "deal" with the other generations, where we found ourselves to be in their midst, in a world we had only read about on album covers. His story is insightful and lets us all know a lot of what went on "behind the curtain" from his perspective during this incredible quick week that has lasted a lifetime.

Rodney Dillard

Leader and voice of legendary group the Dillards, it is Rodney I credit with the fact that I am writing this book and playing music in search of life's Holy Grail. Influencing me at seventeen years old to play bluegrass, when I first saw the Dillards perform in Orange County, he has remained a lifelong mentor and friend, for which I am grateful. Without him, there would not have been this story to tell!

Marty Stuart

The country music star. Marty worked a dozen times with me . . . cheap . . . and we did a few other things besides. Sixteen year-old Marty called me at 5:00 a.m. one morning in a Nashville hotel, saying "McEuen, be in the lobby in twenty minutes" and hung up. He took me to a Lester Flatt breakfast show at WSM radio station (he was playing with Lester Flatt), where I sat in with them at 6:45 a.m. The only song I could think of to play was Earl's "Breakdown." Lester said, "that's a fine number."

Marty has been all over promoting and playing country music his whole life, starting with that teenage gig of playing with Lester. I had him sing "Dreary Black Hills" for the *Music of the Wild West* album many years later. He charged me a dollar. I haven't paid him yet, as he said he wanted to let it "build up." Maybe now?

Steve Martin

A relationship started quizzically in the spring before our high school senior year, when we both landed our dream jobs in Disneyland Magic Shop. My brother started managing him in the 1970s, and Steve and I had taken up banjo by then. Steve was in Nashville during the recording of *Circle* because Bill was recording him with Vassar and Junior for some of his music. Steve and I have known each other and worked together for years; I introduced him to Earl at the sessions.

In 2009 his album, *The Crow: New Songs for the Five-String Banjo*, which I produced, won a Grammy for Best Bluegrass Album of 2009.

Dean Torrence

Dean has a long relationship to Bill McEuen and the NGDB, as a designer he created the album covers for *Uncle Charlie* and *Circle*. Dean was also in the surf music duo Jan and Dean and would go on to form Kitty Hawk Graphics.

Del Bryant

As a longtime Nashville friend (since 1974) and "connected" to the music business, Del has been the president of BMI and guardian of his parents' incredible song catalog. Felice and Boudleaux Bryant, authors of "Rocky Top" and "All I Have to Do Is Dream" (which the NGDB recorded in the

1970s), as well as Everly Brothers hits and countless others. He is recognized as one of the most respected leaders in the music industry.

John Cable

John Cable comes from that group of people who acquired the *Circle* early, got into music, played some NGDB songs, *Circle* songs, and other songs of his own with the Denver band Colors. He was enlisted in NGDB late in the 1970s and went with us on our trip to Russia in 1977. He currently plays with me on the road as part of the String Wizards.

Stuart Duncan

One of America's best fiddlers, I contacted Stuart about giving some words about *Circle* from his viewpoint, as a "younger player" who was enamored by Vassar Clements. Vassar's star shone bright on this album. Credit is due to Earl for making that marriage, because Bill and I did not know the names of who to pick for fiddle. I will never forget Earl's answer to my question of "Can he cover all the styles?" It was "he'll do." Stuart takes that mantle and wears it well. I have had the pleasure of recording with him on several projects, most notably *String Wizards I* and *II*.

Orin Friesen

KFDI Radio Man for forty-four years, Orin has a love of bluegrass that has given him the longest-running bluegrass show on the air—fifty years at this writing! He has been inducted to Kansas Music Hall of Fame; Kansas Bluegrass Hall of Fame; Kansas Cowboy Hall of Fame; and America's Old Time Country Music Hall of Fame and has been a supporter and fan since we started. I used to call him around 2 a.m. to chat on the air, as I had trouble sleeping. He never got tired of it!

Lance Smith

An NGDB agent in the 1970s, Lance worked tirelessly at the new hot business of booking music acts for his agency Stone County, where I spent a lot of off-road time between jobs. Often on the phone with Lance during late hours, I had road managing and band things to keep track of with him. He was like a brother. Lance booked the Earl Scruggs Revue after our introduction to Earl.

From Vanderbilt to Woodland Sound

Gary Scruggs

Gary Scruggs in 1970, the year he and the Scruggs family met the Nitty Gritty Dirt Band.
PHOTO BY AL CLAYTON/COURTESY OF THE AL CLAYTON PHOTOGRAPHY, LLC

In the fall of 1970, I was twenty-one years old in the first semester of my senior year at Vanderbilt University. Vanderbilt is located in Nashville, Tennessee, a dozen or so miles from where my parents, Earl and Louise Scruggs, and younger brothers, Randy and Steve, lived at the time.

When driving my car, I often had the radio tuned in to one of two rock stations in Nashville back then, either WKDA-FM, which was an album-oriented station, or WMAK-AM, which had more of a Top 40 format. I began hearing a record on both stations that grabbed my attention; it was one of those records that will make you want to turn up the volume whenever you hear it on the car radio. There was no sparkling sound of a Rickenbacker electric twelve-string guitar on it, but still, thanks to arpeggiated mandolin fills and high-note piano passages, the record had a "Byrds"-like jingle-jangle aura about it that caught my ear and tugged at my heart.

The song was "Mr. Bojangles," recorded by a band on the rise known as Nitty Gritty Dirt Band. I say "a band on the rise" because I had heard a couple of their previous singles on the radio but not frequently. From the best I can remember, "Mr. Bojangles" was the band's first single to reach coveted "heavy rotation" status on radio stations in Nashville.

Having heard "Mr. Bojangles" several times, I was excited to learn Nitty Gritty Dirt Band would soon be in concert on the Vanderbilt campus. This concert, to be held in Memorial Gymnasium, was scheduled for a weekend date when my father's band, the Earl Scruggs Revue, was not going to be on the road, and I had high hopes of attending. The only obstacle standing in the way was the possibility the Revue would commit to appearing on the *Grand Ole Opry* the evening of this upcoming concert. (The highly acclaimed Flatt & Scruggs partnership, formed in March 1948, had shocked many music fans when Lester Flatt and Earl Scruggs went separate ways in February 1969. Both Lester and Earl formed new bands and retained individual membership as part of the *Opry* cast. My brother Randy and I were members of our father's Earl Scruggs Revue.)

Instead of just picking up the phone, I drove to my parents' home and asked them if we could skip the *Opry* on that particular date so I could attend the Dirt Band's Vanderbilt concert. My mother, who was the Revue's manager after successfully managing Flatt & Scruggs for close to fourteen years, thought about it for a nanosecond and said, "No."

I was disappointed but not surprised to hear her response. Her reasoning, as always, was concise and understandable: We were still trying to become better known and more experienced as a performing act, and the *Grand Ole Opry*—a live radio show held in Nashville's Ryman Auditorium and heard on a far-reaching fifty-thousand-watt radio station (WSM-AM)—was a major platform on which to achieve those goals. Besides, Mom and Dad had never even heard of Nitty Gritty Dirt Band. Still, I kept thinking if only they could hear the "Mr. Bojangles" recording (which I thought sounded way more country than rock), my request might be reconsidered.

When I left the house, I drove to a nearby mom-and-pop record store with the intention of buying a copy of the "Mr. Bojangles" 45-RPM single. It was not in stock; in fact, the store didn't even have it on order at the time, perhaps because the record had not yet started its slow climb up the record charts. ("Mr. Bojangles" would eventually be the Dirt Band's first single to crack the Top 40 in *Billboard* magazine's "Hot 100" chart, peaking at #9 in mid-February 1971.)

But this little record store did have a few copies of the Nitty Gritty Dirt Band album, *Uncle Charlie & His Dog Teddy*. I pulled a copy from one of the record bins, scanned the backside of the album cover, and was happy to see "Mr. Bojangles" listed in the album's collection of songs. My heart then skipped a beat when I noticed one of my father's up-tempo 5-string banjo compositions, "Randy Lynn Rag," was also on the album.

"*BINGO!*" I thought to myself as I placed three or four bucks on the counter to purchase the LP; I sensed the Dirt Band's recording of "Randy Lynn Rag" just might be the deciding factor as to whether the Revue would forgo the *Opry* on the date of the Dirt Band concert.

While on the way back to my parents' home with the *Uncle Charlie* LP in hand, I remember hoping the Dirt Band's version of Dad's song was at least halfway decent; if not, it would surely slam the door on any chance of going to the concert. It occurred to me I should first go to my apartment near Vanderbilt and check out the recorded performance, but instead, I took a giant leap of faith—the "Mr. Bojangles" record was great, so why wouldn't the "Randy Lynn Rag" track also be great? I continued to drive straight to my parents' house.

Upon arriving, I cued up "Mr. Bojangles" on the record player in my mother's home office and played it for Mom and Dad. They seemed to enjoy it. When the song ended, I lifted the record-player needle from the disc and said, "That's by the band coming to Vanderbilt in a few weeks." Other than to say it was a good song and a nice recording, neither Mom nor Dad responded to the not-so-subtle reminder of my wish to skip the *Opry* in favor of going to the Dirt Band's concert. Having heard that lukewarm response, the moment of truth had arrived. I discreetly turned up the volume knob a couple of notches, took a breath, hoped for the best, and said, "Here's another tune you might like." I cued up "Randy Lynn Rag" and when it began to play, both Mom and Dad suddenly smiled widely while listening intently.

I was relieved to find the track was much better than my hoped-for "at least halfway decent." Recorded with a small audience gathered in the recording studio, it had a live, somewhat loose, but feel-good quality about it that was energetic and entertaining. When the instrumental ended, the sound of the small studio audience whooping it up and clapping their hands went on for a few seconds. I recall stifling a laugh (and cringing slightly) when one of the Dirt Band members then said, "Thank you for the clap," but I don't think my mother noticed the comical, but potentially offensive remark.

Dad asked to hear the track again, adding, "Turn it up a little." When the second time around ended, I quickly lifted the needle before the suggestive, "Thank you for the clap" comment could be heard. Mom then said, "When did you say they're playing at Vanderbilt?"

I told her the date and then reminded Mom and Dad I had met and introduced the folk rock band, the Byrds, to them in 1968. The introduction led to Dad, Randy, and I performing with them in a couple of made-for-television filmed recordings, which we all knew would favorably impact both the Earl Scruggs Revue and the Byrds. (The recordings aired on NET [later known as PBS] in January 1971. The Byrds at the time of the recordings were Roger McGuinn, Clarence White, Skip Battin, and Gene Parsons.) I suggested something productive might also come from Dad meeting the Dirt Band. It was decided then and there we would *all* go to the upcoming concert.

By the time the Dirt Band came to Nashville in the fall of 1970, the Earl Scruggs Revue had already performed at Vanderbilt, so I had no trouble arranging for someone on the concert committee to reserve good seats for Mom, Dad, my brothers Randy, Steve, and me, as well as a couple of friends. It had also been arranged for us to meet the Dirt Band in their dressing room if time permitted.

About forty minutes before the concert was to begin, we all met near one of the gymnasium entrances where three parking spaces had been reserved for us. My friend on the concert committee led us to one of the backstage dressing rooms the Dirt Band occupied and knocked on the door. At that time, Dirt Band members were (in last-name alphabetical order) Jimmie Fadden, Jeff Hanna, Jim "Ibby" Ibbotson, John McEuen, and Les Thompson. John McEuen opened the door and welcomed us in. When we entered the room, I was happy to see all the Dirt Banders seemed genuinely excited to meet Earl Scruggs, and they couldn't have been any nicer to the rest of us—and I don't think they were disappointed in Dad's charming and gracious interaction with them.

The introductory meeting didn't last long; the Dirt Band had last-minute preparations before the concert started, and we, the Scruggs family and friends, needed to get to our seats. On our way out of the dressing room, one of the Dirt Banders invited us to come back to the dressing room when the show was over.

We made our way to our seats, and it wasn't long before the house lights dimmed, the band filed onto the stage, and the concert began. The stage, set up on the basketball court around fifteen feet away from the nearest audience members, was wide and high. Sitting in a courtside seat, with several thousand people in attendance, I realized I obviously wasn't the only fan the band had won over with "Mr. Bojangles." I was ready for a good time, and it seemed everyone there had a blast from start to finish.

To my complete surprise, Nitty Gritty Dirt Band opened the concert with my father's composition, "Foggy Mountain Breakdown," which was originally recorded by Flatt & Scruggs in December 1949. Featured prominently in all the chase scenes in the 1967 blockbuster film, *Bonnie and Clyde*, the instrumental was well-known and a surefire crowd-pleaser. Setting the tempo and leading the band along the way, John McEuen picked his 5-string banjo on the lightning-fast tune; Les Thompson played additional leads on mandolin; Ibby Ibbotson strummed a strong rhythm on his acoustic guitar, and mindful of their jug band origins, Jeff Hanna expertly clicked and clawed syncopated licks on his percussive washboard contraption as Jimmie Fadden masterfully navigated his washtub bass. When the tune ended, the revved-up audience responded with thunderous applause and a standing ovation. The band's performance of "Foggy" set the tone for an evening packed full of highlights.

A couple of hours later, I was *more* than surprised when the Dirt Band closed the concert with a reprise of "Foggy Mountain Breakdown"—Mom and Dad were grinning from ear to ear. I believe opening *and* closing the concert with "Foggy Mountain Breakdown" was the Dirt Band's uniquely thoughtful and perfect tip-of-the-hat to Earl Scruggs, knowing he was in the audience. I know it made Dad and the entire family feel great. I was (and still am) so thankful we were all there to enjoy the concert together. That evening remains one of my favorite family memories.

A couple of minutes after the concert ended, we made our way to the Dirt Band's dressing room where a brief jam session began. We sat in a small circle of chairs, talking and laughing between songs. It seemed to me we had known each other forever. Then, all too soon, it was time to go.

As we were leaving, Dad casually said in his soft-spoken and friendly voice, "Maybe we can all record together sometime." Those words may have resonated in more ears than mine, but I don't think any of us had the slightest inkling of what all that night at Vanderbilt would eventually lead to.

Fast-forward several months: A couple of the Dirt Band members and Scruggs family stayed in touch by telephone for those months following the Vanderbilt concert, and friendships began developing. In May 1971, I graduated from Vanderbilt and soon after, Randy graduated from high school. At that point, the Earl Scruggs Revue was able to hit the road in earnest—up until then, our concerts had been primarily restricted to weekends and during school breaks.

After the graduations, one of our first gigs was a five-night stand in June at a popular music venue in Boulder, Colorado, back then called "Tulagi" where we performed two shows a night. In addition to the Revue, Tulagi hosted a diverse variety of acts in the 1970s, including Linda Ronstadt, Bonnie Raitt, John Lee Hooker, Eagles, Doobie Brothers, Miles Davis, Doc Watson, as well as the Dirt Band.

Boulder, which is around thirty miles northwest of Denver, happened to be fairly close to where both John McEuen and Jeff Hanna lived at the time, and they attended some of our shows at Tulagi, even joining us onstage a time or two.

While in Boulder, John formally invited Dad to record with the Dirt Band, and Dad, having already expressed his desire to record with the Dirt Band on the night we all met at Vanderbilt, readily accepted. Soon after the invitation, Nitty Gritty Dirt Band's manager and record producer, William E. "Bill" McEuen (John's older brother), hoped to bring in not only Earl Scruggs, but several of the band's other country music heroes and musical influences as well. The Dirt Banders were all excited about the concept.

My parents were asked to assist in gathering some of those artists to join with the making of the album. Mom and Dad were eager to help. Once preparations started, the yet-to-be-recorded album, *Will the Circle Be Unbroken*, would soon evolve into a colossal triple-disc LP containing more than three dozen songs (recorded in August 1971 at Woodland Sound Studios in East Nashville).

My father, Earl Scruggs, first reached out to Mother Maybelle Carter, who was high on the Dirt Band's wish list of guest artists. She immediately agreed to join in, telling Dad, "If you're gonna be on it, I wanna be on it, too!" Maybelle happened to have been Dad's childhood musical hero, and they had become close friends over the years—and considering she was a member of the original Carter Family that had performed in the famed and historic 1927 Bristol Sessions—Maybelle was literally present for, and participated in, what became known as "the birth of country music."

Dad also introduced Bill McEuen and the Dirt Banders to the *Grand Ole Opry* star Roy Acuff and Roy's music-publishing partner, Wesley Rose. A country-music superstar in the late 1930s and 1940s, Roy was known as "the King of Country Music" despite not having had a Top 5 country hit in more than two decades—and Roy was also known for his staunch conservative views, both political and social.

While Mother Maybelle found it easy to say "Yes" to the project, Dad remembered Roy being reluctant to commit because of his negative view—or perhaps it was distrust—of long-haired young men. The Dirt Band members, all in their early to mid twenties and wore their hair long, and some were bearded as well, which peeved Roy all the more. Dad also vividly remembered Wesley Rose convincing Roy to at least consider taking part when he suggested it would be an easy way of getting a few songs in their Acuff-Rose publishing catalog recorded—that, of course, would mean a windfall of royalty money flowing into the company from record sales and radio play. Roy Acuff may have been perceived by many as being just a hillbilly singer and entertainer, but he could also be a savvy businessman and promoter—and Wesley's verbal nudge seems to have been what it took to get Roy on board with the project.

Once Roy finally agreed to participate, it was a given that Pete "Bashful Brother Oswald" Kirby, who played an integral role in the sound of Roy's band, would play his Dobro guitar on songs Roy sang. Roy's only other requirement was that Earl Scruggs be there to play banjo or guitar on his songs, which Dad was more than happy to do. Dad also played guitar on three instrumental tracks featuring Oswald as well as a couple of Carter Family songs. As for playing 5-string banjo, my father picked his 1930 Gibson Granada on eight songs, including the title track.

In addition to the Earl Scruggs instrumental tunes ("Nashville Blues," "Flint Hill Special," "Earl's Breakdown," and "Soldier's Joy"), the Dirt Band wanted to record bluegrass songs with lyrics, and they hoped bluegrass singer Bill Monroe would be the guest artist to sing the songs of that genre. By 1971, the years-long grudge Monroe had held against his former band members, Lester Flatt and Earl Scruggs, was over. (Monroe was known as "The Father of Bluegrass Music," but it was Flatt & Scruggs, with the help of manager Louise Scruggs, who far outshined Monroe year after year as the most popular and successful bluegrass band in the world. Monroe finally began speaking to both of them again when Flatt & Scruggs split up in 1969.)

Being on friendly terms, my father had no qualms about talking with Monroe on behalf of the Dirt Band. Dad spoke with Monroe and encouraged him to join the project. Monroe flat out rejected the idea, telling Dad he didn't think his fans would "appreciate" him recording with "that kind of people" (a seemingly snide reference to Dirt Band members whose long hair and beards he found unacceptable and controversial; besides, it was rumored Monroe considered them to be nothing more than a hippie rock band that knew absolutely nothing about "his" bluegrass music).

As a result of Monroe's decision to turn down a golden opportunity to expand his popularity to a much wider (and younger record-buying) audience, my mother, Louise, suggested another bluegrass singer, Jimmy Martin, the self-proclaimed "King of Bluegrass," be invited to fill the musical void Monroe's absence created; Mom was helping Martin with a few of his show-date bookings at the time, and he quickly followed her advice to take part in the project.

Perhaps it was fortunate Bill Monroe didn't want to be associated with the Dirt Band members because the often-undisciplined Jimmy Martin, with his exuberant personality, brought an unbridled enthusiasm and energy to the album that Monroe's taciturn and often-stern persona might have dampened, if not drowned.

Dad was also asked to recommend supplemental musicians who could handle upright bass and fiddle parts for the assorted guest artists and their various music styles. He came up with a short list of names. For upright bass, Dad's only recommendation was Nashville's longtime "A-Team" session musician, Roy "Junior" Huskey. Dad's sole recommendation for fiddle was a session player with considerable road experience as a sideman, forty-three-year-old Vassar Clements. (Vassar joined the Earl Scruggs Revue soon after the *Circle* album was completed.)

The Dirt Band wanted the sound of a Dobro guitar in the mix for some of the guest artists, and they had in mind Burkett "Josh" Graves to play that role. Josh had made his mark as a trailblazing Dobroist while playing in Flatt & Scruggs's band, the "Foggy Mountain Boys," for many years. A call was made, but Josh was in Lester Flatt's bluegrass band, "Nashville Grass," at the time, and Flatt did not allow his band members to record with other artists. With Josh unavailable, I believe it was either my mother or father who suggested the super-talented multi-instrumentalist Norman Blake was more than capable of handling the Dobro parts. (Within eight months after declining to take part in the *Circle* project, Josh left Flatt's band and joined Earl's.)

Vassar, Junior, and Norman were hired for the *Circle* sessions. They all performed brilliantly and made such significant contributions to the LP they were given "Also featuring" status on the album's front cover along with Oswald Kirby.

As for the two other iconic guest artists on the Dirt Band wish list, John McEuen personally invited Dad's longtime friend Doc Watson, while Bill McEuen took care of enlisting Merle Travis.

The stage was set, and several weeks later, the Dirt Band arrived in Nashville a few days before the recording sessions began. Rehearsals held at my parents' house felt more like lighthearted picking parties than formal rehearsals, which can feel tedious at times. My brother Randy and I sat in with the others, and the Dirt Band graciously invited both of us to perform on several tracks on the album. Randy played acoustic guitar and autoharp, and I contributed vocal parts.

The feel-good spirit of those living-room rehearsals spilled over into the recording studio once the sessions began. *Circle* was, of course, to be a Nitty Gritty Dirt Band album, but it's interesting to note that the Dirt Banders checked their egos at the door before entering the studio. They were perfectly comfortable taking a back seat and playing supportive roles to the guest artists they so revered. Of thirty-seven songs included on the 1972 release, Dirt Band members were the primary featured vocalist or instrumentalist on just a handful of songs.

Jeff Hanna evoked the memory and musical spirit of Hank Williams when he sang "Honky Tonk Blues"; Ibby Ibbotson soulfully rendered "Lost Highway"; Jimmie Fadden's version of "Honky Tonkin'" was both understated and whimsical; John McEuen picked rapid-fire notes on the 5-string banjo as he showcased his recent composition "Togary Mountain."

As individuals, no Dirt Bander was so vain as to think he had to perform on every single song; according to liner credits, all five band members appeared at the same time on only a dozen or so of the many tracks. The Dirt Banders might have been the out-of-towners, but in the Woodland studio, they played perfect hosts to all the Nashvillians involved in the project.

As for the songs sung by Jeff, Ibby, and Jimmie—all three were originally made famous by the legendary Hank Williams. Perhaps choosing to sing those particular songs was the Dirt Band's subliminal way of saying Hank would have been invited to be a guest artist on the *Circle* album had he not died tragically on New Year's Day 1953 at the age of twenty-nine.

Released in early 1972, no hit singles resulted from *Circle*—deemed "too country" by many mainstream country music radio stations, the album got much more airplay on less-stringent "underground" FM stations. *Circle* created a buzz, and through word-of-mouth promotion, its popularity spread. The bottom line is that a lot of people heard it, liked it, and bought it. *Circle* eventually peaked at #4 on the *Billboard* country albums chart.

Circle was certainly a healthy shot in the arm for Roy Acuff and Acuff-Rose publishing, just as Wesley Rose had predicted—most of the seven songs featuring either Roy or Oswald were Acuff-Rose copyrights, along with several other songs under the Acuff-Rose umbrella featuring other *Circle* artists. Roy's plaintive and emotion-packed vocals heard on *Circle* informed many people why he had been dubbed "the King of Country Music."

When on the road with the Earl Scruggs Revue, a period of time seemed to fly by when I saw more and more of Mother Maybelle Carter performing at music festivals with her band of talented grandchildren. I recall Maybelle crediting the increased demand for her appearances to her participation on the *Circle* album.

Vassar Clements quickly gained new and widespread recognition following the release of *Circle*, which helped enable him to launch his own solo career around the beginning of 1973.

Circle also lent credence to Earl Scruggs's growing reputation as an older artist who sincerely embraced the talents, opinions, and spirit of much younger musicians. Dad was forty-seven years old during the *Circle* sessions, but still, he was almost twenty-one years younger than Roy Acuff, fifteen years younger than Maybelle Carter; so he was, in fact, a generational bridge connecting the Dirt Band "boys" to the elderly Roy and Maybelle. To my father, having already performed with younger artists such as Bob Dylan, Joan Baez, and the Byrds, those experiences were fresh and exciting, and he wanted to continue having new musical adventures, and recording with the Dirt Band was certainly one of his most noted experiences.

In the era of the late 1960s and early 1970s, growing social, cultural, and generational gaps had become highly politicized and polarizing; it was older folks' traditional values versus young people's more liberal lifestyles, rednecks versus hippies, Vietnam War advocates versus Vietnam War protesters, and so on. As a result of such divides, *Circle* was a leap of faith for some of the guest artists as well as Nitty Gritty Dirt Band. The Dirt Banders, who were just then coming off their breakthrough Top 10 pop hit, "Mr. Bojangles," elected to roll the dice and dive head-first into a recording project featuring older country music artists, some of whom were totally unknown to many of their young fans.

During this time of heightened division, suspicion, and uncertainty, *Circle* proved people of different generations and different social and cultural backgrounds can come together and produce something positive and appealing to folks of all ages and from all walks of life.

The *Circle* album was eventually followed by *Will the Circle Be Unbroken* volumes two (released in 1989), and three (2002). Even though *Circle 3* includes "The Lowlands"—a song I coincidentally wrote during that pivotal senior year at Vanderbilt—it's the *Circle 1* album I think of as monumental. It introduced a mixture of various country music styles of the 1930s, 1940s, and 1950s with bluegrass music and what became known as "Americana" music to Dirt Band fans who otherwise might never have become knowledgeable and appreciative of those musical genres. At the same time, it introduced fans of Maybelle, Earl, Acuff, Martin, Doc, and Merle to the Dirt Band.

Earl Scruggs meeting Nitty Gritty Dirt Band at Vanderbilt University in 1970 did not lead to an end of all wars or a creation of a new and better world order. But it did lead to *Will the Circle Be*

Unbroken, an iconic work of art with the title song suggesting hope can replace despair, and common ground exists for us all, whether we walk upon it, or are buried beneath it.

I'm grateful for John McEuen inviting me to contribute to this book showcasing his brother's photographs. I've thoroughly enjoyed reviewing the pictures, listening to the *Circle* tracks, and recalling many precious memories of an ever-expanding circle of family and friends. Such memories are well worth revisiting from time to time.

—Gary Scruggs

The Scruggs Family at the Country Music Hall of Fame and Museum, 2004. (Left to right, sitting): Earl Scruggs and Louise Scruggs; (standing): Gary Scruggs and Randy Scruggs.
PHOTO BY DONN JONES FORTHE COUNTRY MUSIC HALL OF FAME AND MUSEUM

Rodney Dillard

Rodney Dillard, founder of the Dillards

Rodney Dillard
PHOTO BY ANTHONY LADD, KNEELINDESIGN.COM

John McEuen became interested in the 5-string banjo when he heard my brother Doug Dillard play the banjo in a club in California, the Paradox, when the Dillards first came from the Ozarks to LA around 1963.

In the 1960s the music scene was looking for new identity after the folk craze faded into the museum of musical moments. A group of young men, including John McEuen and Les Thompson, formed a band called the Nitty Gritty Dirt Band.

With the help of his brother Bill, the Dirt Band established a hybrid sound of second-generation country and West Coast pop music. This brought them on the major music scene with several hit records. Looking for a career move that would establish the group as a musical icon, the McEuen brothers came up with a recording event that would make music history and expose traditional music to a broader audience, the audience of colleges and concerts. It also archived, for future generations, the artists who laid the foundation for country music, in their album we all know as the *Circle* album. It created for other bluegrass and country artists the opportunity to increase their fan base and made *Will the Circle Be Unbroken* a financial blockbuster.

—Rodney Dillard

The Kindness of Strangers
(with Regards from the Outer Edge of Nashville)

Marty Stuart, Country Music Performer

Marty Stuart
PHOTO COURTESY ANTHONY SCARLATI

Country music is approaching the one-hundred-year milestone of its recorded existence. Of all the landmark events associated with the evolution of country music, the Nitty Gritty Dirt Band's *Will the Circle Be Unbroken* stands as one of the culture's most sacred and profound documents. *Will the Circle Be Unbroken* lives on and continually inspires in an Old Testament kind of way. The artwork on the cover, the bold statement of a three-album set, the photography, as well as the storied welcoming of young, forward-thinking outsiders into the inner family of a well-guarded, conservative empire all suggest an artistically adventurous, harmonious summit between new and old-world musical orders. The end result of the *Circle* proceedings bore witness of timeless music, goodwill, unrestricted freedom of expression, love, and honor.

At the point in time when the *Circle* sessions occurred, the state of the country music union was the rhinestoned fiddle and steel sounds of the 1950s and 1960s were in decline. Miles above the roots, lushly arranged, soft-edged, polite country pop songs were being promoted in an effort to achieve broader demographics for an ambitious country music industry. The outlaw side of town was beginning to rumble and question corporate musical authority. There was an abundance of singer-songwriters making the rounds up and down Nashville's Music Row. Bluegrass music was unknowingly on the edge of expansion. Johnny Cash hosted a weekly network television show that was making strides in eradicating musical boundaries. The *Grand Ole Opry* was still going fifty-thousand-watts strong every Friday and Saturday night, and people such as Roy Acuff, Bashful

Brother Oswald, Mother Maybelle Carter, Doc Watson, Merle Travis, Norman Blake, Vassar Clements, Jimmy Martin, Junior Huskey, and Earl Scruggs were regarded as royal but time-worn heroes from days gone by. In what appeared to be a radical and most unlikely pairing, the aforementioned people joined forces with ragtag Colorado rock stars known as the Nitty Gritty Dirt Band with the idea in mind of making music together. What most of the world did not know was how much these rockers loved and championed American roots music and its creators.

The McEuen brothers pitched the concept of *Will the Circle Be Unbroken* to Liberty Records. After getting the mighty green light, John McEuen booked Earl Scruggs and Doc Watson. Beyond that, on the strength of handshakes and a few "these boys are alright" phone calls placed by Earl and Louise Scruggs, time was booked at Woodland Studios on the east side of Nashville and the recording sessions began. In six days' time, the Nitty Gritty Dirt Band captured the heart and soul of country music. They waded out into the eternal waters and experienced moments that undoubtably became treasured keepsakes that've been kept close to the heart ever since.

When *Will the Circle Be Unbroken* was released, everybody won. It was a rogue hit. The music industry did not see it coming. The band succeeded in following their hearts and fulfilling their vision, which resulted in recordings that were heralded as "worthy of spiritual comparison to the Bristol Sessions of 1927." The artists and musicians who participated experienced fresh notoriety and energized careers, as well as the acceptance of a contemporary generation of enthusiastic followers. Critics praised the project, the cash register rang, the record company smiled, and it was all in the name of authenticity.

In truth, country music came off the launching pad of those 1927 Bristol Sessions looking for mass appeal and pop star acclaim. As country artists, we are at our best when we're at home with our natural selves. However, throughout the years we've been guilty, way more than once, of watering down our authentic selves to make our music more palatable to the multitudes. The record shows that it has often been the fond gaze of notable people from outside the walls of country music who've recognized the beauty and relevance of what we often overlook or leave behind while in search of more lucrative pastures. The kindness of strangers has often led us back home.

Bob Dylan shined the light on the Nashville skyline and its mighty "A-team" of musicians on some of his late-1960s Columbia recordings. A parade of his peers followed suit and experienced working with many of the brilliant minds who collectively defined the term "Nashville cats." The Byrds proclaimed the power of country music on the adventurous *Sweetheart of the Rodeo*. Films such as *Bonnie and Clyde, Deliverance*, and *O Brother, Where Art Thou* are to be considered gifts that were handed down from another world. Rock-and-roll visionary Jack White leveraged his star power to produce and reconfirm the absolute greatness of the "coal miner's daughter," Loretta Lynn, in the autumn of her career. Mega producer and hip-hop and rock-and-roll mogul Rick Rubin afforded country music's Man in Black, Johnny Cash, a late-life victory lap which he otherwise might never have known. The only record label I could find that recognized the power in what was to be Porter Wagoner's final recording was the LA-based, predominantly punk, Anti Records. America's premier documentarian, Ken Burns, along with producer Dayton Duncan, turned their attention toward the culture of country music in the form of a 16½-hour series that tells the story of country music with a brevity like never before. Thanks to these men, country music is now in the same room with baseball, the National Parks, the Civil War, the Roosevelts, and Jazz. As time goes on the world of country music will no doubt have more stories such as these to tell. However, I do believe when it's all said and done, that the moment in time when the Nitty Gritty Dirt Band offered their hearts to Mr. Acuff, Brother Oswald, Norman Blake, Mother Maybelle, Doc, Vassar, Merle Travis, Junior Huskey, King Jimmy and Earl . . . the world was at its best. As the song says, "Everything Was Beautiful." What we are left with from those six days is *Will the Circle Be Unbroken*, and it's bound to be remembered as the King of Them All.

Marty Stuart

Congress of Country Music

Philadelphia, Mississippi

The *Circle* Album Cover

Steve Martin, Comedian, Banjo Picker

COURTESY OF DANNY CLINCH

For a dozen or more years in my early career, I had a manager. His name was Bill McEuen, and when I signed on in 1968, we both admitted that we really didn't know what a manager did. We both knew, however, that the words "champion," "advocate," and "believer," were in there somewhere. Bill's look was "cowboy/hippie," and it never changed up to his death in 2020, though it could be argued that it became "Hawaiian/cowboy," as he moved to Hawaii one year and never came back.

I met Bill because in high school I had heard that his younger brother, John McEuen, played the banjo, with which I had an increasing fascination. I sought out John, and my life changed. My first meeting with Bill was at their family home in Garden Grove, California, around 1961. Bill brought in his guitar and flat picked "In the Jailhouse Now," by Jimmie Rodgers, crooning the lyrics with an acquired twang. Bill's mother would interrupt, saying, "Use your pretty voice."

Bill was meticulous about album cover art. He represented the Nitty Gritty Dirt Band and pored over the details of each new release obsessively. In 1970, he showed me the mock-up for the cover of the band's new album, *Uncle Charlie & His Dog Teddy*. He made sure I was aware of the embossing, the metallic shine of the cursive lettering, and the fidelity to the original antique photo of the actual Uncle Charlie. Bill could spend an hour sensually trailing his hand across the "chrome coat board," the proposed album material. He spoke the words "chrome coat board" with the same reverential inflection that a believer might use to speak of the True Cross.

Bill's use of a recorded interview with the real Uncle Charlie—a relative of Bill's wife Alice—was certainly a precursor to the recorded dialogue of the *Circle*'s illuminati that graces its tracks.

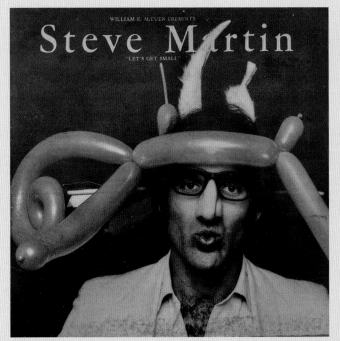

Steve Martin albums produced by Bill McEuen

I had spent a few weeks in Nashville while the album was being recorded, tagging along on the leftover studio hours to record my own banjo tunes, getting free time with the great bassist Junior Huskey, the master fiddler Vassar Clements, and a few other renowned players on the *Circle* album who indulged me for fun.

Bill then went to work on the cover art. He was assisted by Dean Torrence, an art director whose history as a cofounder of the rock group Jan and Dean gave him special status. I'm sure Bill loved the idea that it was a three-record set, as it gave him more surface area to appease his fixation on album art. It was the days before the internet, but Bill somehow dug up a steel engraving of Union general David Porter and flanked him with an array of US flags and Confederate flags, which, to Bill, represented the unification of the country rather than an awful division, completing the "Circle" of reunion.

Bill enlisted his wife, Alice McEuen, to do the expert calligraphy on the inside and back of the album; this was a rare talent to be found among the drugged-out citizens of Laurel Canyon in the 1970s. Alice knew almost everyone on the album, which was intimately and delicately expressed in the sweeping curves of her longhand.

As we all know, the album became a classic and the cover iconic. I'm sure Bill lost a little part of him when the microscopic album art of the CD came into being but might have been buoyed by the resurgence of the LP in recent years. Bill's dedication to the details showed in the rest of the music career, as well as his extensive film career.

Dean Torrence

The Story behind the Design of the *Circle* Album

Dean Torrence

Bill McEuen arrived at my super eclectic design studio on Sunset Boulevard right in the epicenter of the West Coast music scene. Bill was aware of my history as a pretty successful recording artist who just happened to be on the same record label that he had just signed a record deal with. He had heard somewhere that I had complained about my relationship with that company's art department. As a recording artist, I was frustrated that I could not get the art director of that record company's art department to sit down with me and talk about how to translate our beach, or car culture lifestyle music into a visual experience, so when a consumer was listening to our music they could also have a visual component that complimented our music, seemed pretty obvious to me, but not to him. I was told many times, "you make the music and we will make the art."

Sadly, my music partner Jan Berry was critically injured in an automobile accident, and our recording careers were over, and I now was a graphic designer who became an advocate for recording artists (mostly my old friends) who were having the same problems I had on my record label. I became the liaison between the recording artist and the record company and the art department. Now mind you, executives at a record company needed to keep their recording artists happy, the recording artists were keeping the company in business, not some old fart in the art department. So my advice to my recording artist friends or new clients was for them to go straight to the president of the record company's office and demand that they wanted an independent contractor to do their graphic design materials and that was me. That was why Bill McEuen showed up at my door.

Bill had already had that meeting with the president of the company and he and his staff were all on board with Bill's vision, so we went right to work

We were competing with a lot of rock superstars who all had high brand recognition, and we were trying to promote a ragtag bunch of young guys who played banjos, mandolins, harmonicas, and acoustic guitars and sang country music. Bill and I both believed in "perceived value," so everything we did looked like the Nitty Gritty Dirt Band belonged in the mix with all the other successful rock stars. Their packaging would be exquisite, the photography would be perfect, the design would be clean and creative, and even the paper for all of this was to be printed on will be custom paper. This was our wish list; now, we needed to implement our vision.

The first cover we worked on was *Uncle Charlie & His Dog Teddy*. On the cover, we featured the real Uncle Charlie and his dog Teddy. He is holding an acoustic guitar, so the music fan will know that this is probably a country music album, but at the same time it doesn't look like the typical country music album. Bill and I wanted to make the statement visually that this was a pop-country music album, but for sure, the roots of the music came from the past, that is why Uncle Charlie was on the cover. Now we needed to work on the Nitty Gritty Dirt Band branding. So, I first worked on the logo. I always liked to find a recognizable (conscious or subconscious) first letter. I had done this before with the Chicago band logo, the capital "C" was from the Coca-Cola logo. I had always liked the Nesbitt's orange soda pop logo, so I borrowed the capital "N" and went on from there. Once I had all the lettering and decorative borders done, I had an etched zinc plate made of my design. Then I hand-painted the background Hershey chocolate brown and sanded the paint off the lettering and the borders. Next, I inserted Uncle Charlie's picture that I had sepia toned. The finished art was all earth tones, or you could say rich dirt tones.

Bill and I hand delivered the two (front and back cover) painted zinc plates to the color separator, who would then make the four-color film that would then be sent to the album cover printing plant. A few days later, we were informed that the four-color proofs were ready for us to view. When we saw these proofs, we rejected them because the brown was not the same Hershey brown that was on our artwork. To them it was brown, but to us it was the wrong brown; there was too much red, a mahogany color, and we wanted chocolate brown, rich dirt brown. Please do another proof! They were not happy about having to start all over because they were used to mostly minor changes. A few days later we were told that the new proofs are ready for our approval and guess what, we didn't approve the second set of film proofs either. Yes, the red was gone but now there is too much blue, kind of drab olive brown, for sure this was not chocolate brown. Please do it again and do not call us until the proof looks like chocolate. This is a "Dirt" Band album cover. Got the call for the third approval try, and it was spot on. Bill later gave them a gold record and a copy of the Grammy Nomination for Album Cover of the year. All is well that ends well!

Not only did we get to do everything we hoped to do with our covers, but we also even got more! Some of our covers were dye cut; some were embossed; and there was a cover that had a fifth custom color because we didn't like the normal process red color, so we added a Chinese Red on top of the process red. We even printed biographies and reviews on the usually blank white dustcover sleeves that covered the records. We didn't waste any surface. We had a story to tell, and we needed that extra space.

Did you ever think you would see Nitty Gritty Dirt Band and exquisite in the same sentence? A juxtaposition? Actually most of our covers were in the juxtaposition style if you think about it.

Bill and I did two Nitty Gritty Dirt Band album covers that got Nominations for the Best Album Cover of the Year, *Uncle Charlie & His Dog Teddy* (1970) and *Dream* (1975). We didn't win a Grammy for either cover, but we were thrilled to be in the conversation. Now I did win a Grammy for a cover I designed in 1971 that I thought really sucked; the Dirt Band covers were so much better!

One day Bill arrived at my funky design studio with the newest project. I was thinking how we could beat anything we had already done. Bill had the answer. A three-record set (never been done before) featuring some of the best classic and beloved country musicians and songwriters from the past who would be playing with some of their biggest fans, the Nitty Gritty Dirt Band. This design would be tricky. We couldn't make this package too contemporary, or we might have offended the older classic country music fan base, but it needed to look at least contemporary enough so that the Dirt Band fans would be interested enough to pony up the extra bucks to buy this unusual package. Most all this music came from the Deep South, so we came up with an etching of a Civil War general in a cool etched oval. I added the Confederate flags and the American flags. Yes, there was a Civil War but in the end the Circle was not broken. I did most of the lettering on the cover, and Bill's wife Alice did the title lettering. Bill took the pictures and Alice did the hand lettering on the back cover. Either Bill or Alice singed the paper, and it didn't go well the first time they did it, but they finally did one that was readable. The inside had three pockets for the three vinyl records, and it took some dye cutting to make it happen. Bill included more than forty photos that he had taken documenting the recording sessions in the creating the music for the *Circle* album. He wanted these photos to look more like snapshots than a planned-out photo shoot with perfect lighting. He wanted to tell a visual story about music, friends, and life, so there were photos that reflected that country lifestyle as well. He even included a black-and-white photo of an old antique WSM radio station mixing board and asked me to splice in a current photo of the Dirt Band and other musicians in the studio in the background so it looked like that old mixing board was used in recording of the album. I also spent a lot of time "sepia toning" that photo, so it looked really old. I really liked how it turned out. There was a ton of copy contained in this package, everything from lengthy credits to reviews. There was also a poster included.

Will the Circle Be Unbroken sold more than a million copies; I have a gold record on my wall that Bill gave me, and I am proud of that gold record! And thank you Bill for those two album cover design nominations because those awards cemented my credibility of a legit graphic designer and for that I will always be grateful.

Miss you soooo much!

PS Not so bad for a ragtag bunch of young guys from LA

Dean Torrence, Kitty Hawk Graphics, formerly of surf music duo Jan & Dean

Del Bryant, Past BMI President, Music Maven, Nice Guy . . .

Del Bryant
PHOTO COURTESY CAROLYN BRYANT
PHOTO BY JOHN McEUEN

On Monday, October 2, 1972, wearing the first suit and tie that I'd ever purchased, I began working at Broadcast Music, Inc.—BMI—on Nashville's Music Row. The Vietnam War, winding down, had divided the country; fueled by brutal racial enmity, cities had burned. The chasm between longhairs and rednecks seemed immeasurable. That year, *Will the Circle Be Unbroken* bridged genres and generations through the powerful unity of music.

I remember my amazement at the brilliant authenticity of this unlikely kinship between the California band and the country and bluegrass legends they invited to join them. And I recall being equally surprised that millions of record buyers—many if not most of them dedicated rock fans—were in agreement. Fifty years later, this album endures as one of the most monumental collaborations in the history of modern music.

Throughout my childhood, I spent almost every weekend backstage with my family at the Grand Ole Opry, from the late 1940s on. My parents, Felice and Boudleaux Bryant, were a legendary songwriting team, probably best known for the Tennessee state song "Rocky Top," and the Everly Brothers hits, "All I Have to Do Is Dream," and "Bye Bye Love," among a repertoire of more than fifteen hundred songs. From their early cuts like "Out Behind the Barn" for Little Jimmy Dickens, they penned a catalog of hits for country stars like Hank Snow and Ernest Tubb among a roster of iconic artists that includes Elvis Presley, the Beatles, Bob Dylan, Ray Charles, and Buddy Holly.

I came of age surrounded by the legends of country music as guests in our home or as guests in theirs. Hearing Roy Acuff and the Carter Family with Mother Maybelle from the wings of the Ryman Auditorium, I had witnessed history personified by harmonies in songs that echoed from the hills and hollows of Appalachia. This music was the heritage of hardscrabble lives, accompanying jubilant whiskey-soaked festivities and sorrowful processions of hand-carved coffins, with the chorus of a "Better home awaiting in the sky," promising a triumphant eternity. Then as now, lyrics and melodies portrayed a living legacy.

Looking back through a lens of fifty years, it is resoundingly clear that it was no small task assembling this remarkable cast of musicians. It is truly a testament to the warmth that John McEuen and the members of the Nitty Gritty Dirt Band radiated in persuading these momentous musicians, in the spirit of a family reunion, to try something new. In doing so, the band bestowed on these legends a profound mantle of respect and reverence. Half a century later, this incandescent collection continues to reflect the brightest light of American music.

—Del Bryant

John Cable, Member of NGDB 1975–1978

John Cable
PHOTO COURTESY JOHN CABLE

My musical journey started with the folk movement of the early 1960s. Being from Texas, I was also drawn to the traditional styles of what is now considered Americana and the country music of the 1950s–1960s. I didn't really see any new artists who sounded like the Wilburn Brothers or the bands that played Panther Hall in Fort Worth on a Friday night. But all of a sudden, there was Buffalo Springfield, Poco, the Dillards and the Nitty Gritty Dirt Band. These guys were taking the traditional sounds and turning them upside down. I loved it! NGDB captured my attention with the Michael Nesmith song "Some of Shelley's Blues" and, of course, "Mr. Bojangles." But, in 1972 they took a giant leap in my estimation with the release of *Will the Circle Be Unbroken*. There they were with the giants of early country music and the Grand Ole Opry. Musicians that had informed my playing and singing for years. It was a deep dive into the history of our music in America that is timeless and everlasting. It was also quite a risk for the boys. That is what I so admired. Three years later, I joined a Texas band that moved to Colorado and signed a booking contract with the Dirt Band's agent. They put us on the road opening for NGDB, and I couldn't believe my luck. I became friends with all of them and am to this day. When they asked me to join them in 1975, I jumped at the chance. Not just to play with them, but to pick up what I could from their experiences during those historical recordings. I can still listen to that record to this day and feel like I did when it first came to my attention.

John McEuen has recruited me to play in his new band, the String Wizards. We spend a good portion of our show on the songs from the first *Circle* album. Those songs still touch so many people. They smile with recognition and begin to sing along, and they are great fun to play. Our shows have an intimate, communal feel that is rare these days. I thank all the boys for allowing me into the "circle." It has given me quite a ride! I expect that *Will the Circle Be Unbroken* will be around for a long, long time.

—John Cable, 2021

Stuart Duncan, Nashville Fiddler Extraordinaire

Circle arrived tucked under my father's arm one day in 1972. It was the same year I started to play the fiddle.

My dad played some banjo, so I was the smartest seven-year-old in my class when it came to Earl Scruggs. I had also just witnessed a Scruggs Revue show featuring Vassar Clements. For years my father would tell the story of his heart racing worriedly when Vassar handed me his iconic violin to hold for him as he went to get coffee over a bare concrete floor.

Earl and Vassar were for me the gateway guys toward understanding the *Circle*.

I rapidly became familiar with the other giants featured. Just two years later, I played a guest spot on the *Grand Ole Opry* with a kids' band. When Roy Acuff rounded the corner backstage, I knew who he was because of the *Circle* album.

Awareness of the longevity of old-time musical and cultural traditions is not usually a focus point in public school. I think this recording provided that for me. Because of this historic undertaking, the perceived obstacles to generations and cultures intermingling went up in smoke. Suddenly here was an amalgamation of hippies and hillbillies layin' it down together.

I believe the honesty of the interplay during and in between songs, and the clarity of the recording will stand as a benchmark and changing point for "live in the studio recording."

In anticipation of these thoughts, and because of my reaction, my father drove back to the record store and bought a second copy, which remains unopened to this day.

Stuart Duncan, fiddler

Orin Friesen, KFDI radioman, "Ranch Hand"

Orin Friesen
PHOTO COURTESY AARON BOWEN

Though the Nitty Gritty Dirt Band had been around since 1966, it was their 1971 release, *Uncle Charlie & His Dog Teddy*, with its three hit singles that finally gave the band its big break. *Charlie* proved that these guys were not only a great rock-and-roll band, but that they were also skilled in playing bluegrass and traditional country. *Uncle Charlie* was a springboard into the future and led to the landmark album, *Will the Circle Be Unbroken.*

The band's producer/manager, Bill McEuen, and his brother John (band member) had the idea to take those bluegrass and traditional country elements, displayed in *Uncle Charlie*, and make an acoustic album, knowing that it would be important but would also likely keep the band off the radio for a while. Despite lacking "hit singles," *Circle* remains one of the band's outstanding successes.

For me, *Will the Circle Be Unbroken* is not only *one* of the most important record albums in the history of country music, it is *the* most important record album in the history of country music. If Ralph Peer's Bristol Sessions were the "big bang" of country music, *Will the Circle Be Unbroken* is one of the major aftershocks.

There is a lot of great music on *Circle*, but the project's significance transcends the recording of the music itself. This wasn't the first time that long-haired California rock and rollers had played country music. The Byrds recorded *Sweetheart of the Rodeo*, another one of my favorite albums, which was a bold attempt and an artistic success. Though the Byrds went so far as to record in Nashville, as had Bob Dylan, they went there as the "stars" of the project, using the talents of a few Nashville session players. When the Nitty Gritty Dirt Band went to Nashville to make the *Circle* album, they went not only to pay tribute to their musical heroes but also to make music with them on an equal level and hoped to be accepted among those legendary pickers and singers. They were. The Dirt Band guys didn't go to Nashville to record with sidemen, they *were* the sidemen going to record with the "stars." Even on the album cover, they gave themselves lesser billing than their guest performers, featured on the left side. Egos set aside for the greater good? Now there's a concept!

I had been attending bluegrass music festivals for a couple of years, but a few months after the release of *Will the Circle Be Unbroken*, I went to Winfield, Kansas, for the first of the Walnut Valley Festivals. Though still mostly a bluegrass festival at the time, the event brought together performers as diverse as Lester Flatt and New Grass Revival. The occasion was also billed as the National Guitar Flat-Picking Championship and was highlighted by an onstage jam led by flat-picker Dan Crary and the two main flat pickers from the *Circle* album, Norman Blake and Doc Watson. The Kerrville Folk Festival also began in 1972, and Telluride came along the following year. The growing success of *Circle* and the acceptance of its music spread, and young people were drawn to these new types of music festivals, not only to see and hear the performers onstage but also to learn and to make music of their own, with friends and strangers, young and old . . . to put aside their differences for common enjoyment. Credit must go to the Nitty Gritty Dirt Band for being a catalyst to making this happen.

Will the Circle Be Unbroken is much more than an excellent collection of songs and instrumentals. It is a bridge between the cultures of the liberal Southern California youth and the conservative music standard bearers of the American Southeast. Fifty years later, the *Circle* album still points the way as to how things can be if diverse cultures and political idealities come together by doing something they both enjoy . . . .by making music together. May the Circle once again be complete and forever remain unbroken.

—Orin Friesen

International Bluegrass Music Awards Show Producer,

bass player, fifty years broadcasting bluegrass radio

Lance Smith, Former NGDB Agent

Lance Smith
PHOTO COURTESY LANCE SMITH

In a recent conversation with John, he told me that he was working on a project to commemorate the fiftieth anniversary of the release of *Will the Circle Be Unbroken.* I said "What? How did we get so old?"

John and Bill spent time formalizing plans for a project bringing the rock 'n roll world of California and the Nitty Gritty Dirt Band together with the pure country and bluegrass segments of the music industry. What could be easier than putting a bunch of long-haired hippies in a recording studio with the most traditional and storied performers ever? It was not easy. First, somebody from the traditional side had to agree that this coming together could be important. On top of that, it had never been done before.

Since I was already working with the NGDB as part of their booking team, I got information a little earlier than most. I learned that Earl Scruggs had agreed to participate and that others would soon be on board. Studios were booked, sessions were planned, and it all began.

John decided that more needed to be done and *Circle* changed my life again. When I say "changed my life," I mean way to the upside on all levels. It was time for me to meet Earl and his Revue. So, it was off to Nashville for me. The goal, of course, was to get Earl more comfortable with his new acquaintances (me as agent) and more involved with the whole process as John and Bill visualized it. To summarize so far, we have long-haired hippie Californians (NGDB), a long-haired hippie agent from Denver—to Nashville—the music capital of the world, and tradition; plus, there was the wild card—Louise. Yes, Mrs. Scruggs was manager to the aforementioned.

Bill informed me that the meeting was set for the following morning at the home of Earl and Louise. He let me know that I was to be there at 7:30 a.m. I got there on time and rang the doorbell and instantly felt under a giant microscope. In front of me were Earl, Louise, Randy, and Gary Scruggs. I think they thought I was an alien. We talked for about an hour, specifically about our agency and our peripheral involvement with the *Circle* album. Afterward, Louise served us all a traditional country breakfast. I left happy, full, and Earl's new agent.

People are funny if you have not figured it out. The massive three-album set was not completely packaged or distributed yet. But people were talking about it, and they needed their piece of the action. Earl Scruggs was a superstar who helped make the *Circle* album happen. The *Circle* album did not create the superstar, but it sure reinforced it, while creating a whole new generation of believers.

The Revue—Earl, Gary, Randy Scruggs, Vassar Clements, and Josh Graves—was ready to go. We started by doing a couple of NEC conventions. For those of you that have never heard of this organization, it consisted of colleges and universities throughout the country. Each school had its own body that arranged for concerts, lectures, and speakers for the academic year. For concerts they would have a showcase and each act would have twenty to twenty-five minutes to sell themselves. Many tours were established, and careers made through this organization. It may not sound like much, but it is where I met Waylon Jennings, Jimmy Buffett, Seals and Crofts, Bruce Springsteen, and many more. Earl Scruggs was made for it, and the Revue quickly gained acceptance in this arena.

While Earl was adapting to his new stardom on college campuses, we began to hear from a new set of unexpected outlets clamoring for the Earl Scruggs Revue, places like the Boarding House in San Francisco, Ebbets Field in Denver, the Cowtown Ballroom in Kansas City, and the Great Southeast Music Hall in Atlanta. All were interested in booking the Revue. These were not his normal venues. They were hip and young and featured a lot of rock bands—not acoustic bluegrass bands.

I will never forget one night at the Great Southeast Music Hall (in Atlanta). Earl was the headliner, and Louise was there to see what this sold-out crowd was like. One of my great failings was I wanted to listen to the bands I worked with. Louise, on the other hand, thought that when Earl played, it was time to do business. Earl goes on stage to a thunderous ovation and, Louise drags me to the dressing room to have one of those "if you can't get it done, I will get someone who can" moments. We are in the midst of this one-sided discussion, the band is playing, and the door to the dressing room flies open. There stands Earl in the doorway with a big grin on his face. He politely says, "dang it, I broke a string just when I was going to do good!" as he thanked me for the gig. That ended the meeting.

With *Will the Circle Be Unbroken* now released, the NGDB went back out on the road. The album itself was a tremendous success—both artistically and financially. In fact, it is still selling today. The

NGDB is still on the road some fifty years later playing to crowds of old fans, as well as the new ones created in part by the generations of music lovers who found them through this album.

Earl's career took a huge upswing through his participation in the album giving an untold number of fans' music lovers, and other artists an insight into what can happen when two different worlds collaborate on a single purpose. In this case, it was music. So, who benefited the most? I would like to think that we all did. If you know the history, you know that generations have been influenced. Earl continued playing to the end.

AFTERWORD

JOHN McEUEN

Reflection on William E. McEuen (1941–2020)

Reflecting on my brother, Bill. He was my father figure in many ways, since ours passed on at age fifty-two. Bill was five years older than me. We each thought, as we approached that landmark fifty-second year, our time was near, but it would not be for a while. When he put together the *Circle* sessions, he had not yet made any movies, at which he would be successful. I introduced him to Steve Martin, a budding comedian friend. We met just before senior high school year in Garden Grove, California, and worked in Disneyland together for the best three years a teenager could have. It took a few years for Steve to take off, but Bill pushed, and it worked. The details are in my book, *The Life I've Picked*, the story told from my viewpoint.

After *Circle*, Bill had in front of him: *The Jerk* (and several other Steve Martin movies), producing four albums with Steve that sold about 9½ million units, *Pee-Wee's Big Adventure; The Big Picture; Pee-Wee's Big Top*; and *Pulse.* They were all studio pictures for which he was executive producer with his company, Aspen Film Society.

Self-portrait by Bill McEuen

Bill was a guiding hand in NGDB albums from the *Uncle Charlie & His Dog Teddy,* through the 1970s, making the deals with Liberty and then United Artists. Along the way he produced and managed other artists, and with *Charlie* in 1969, he started producing our records.

I miss Bill. When he was managing NGDB (until he and I passed his duties on to Chuck Morris about 1981), he had great ideas about what we should do, and we worked as a team. We did some of them, and they worked. We should have done more together, but life is hard to . . . control.

For *Circle*, Bill and I (my part was initially getting Earl and Doc to say "yes") had to go together to the president of Liberty Records, Mike Stewart, to get the money to record. Bill did his pitch, I did mine . . . we were really good! I explained to Mike how "when we play colleges, people don't know who Doc, Earl, Travis, Maybelle, Jimmy Martin are. Much of our music comes from their influence; we do some of their songs and we have to let our audience know about them! I think they would be interested. They would eat them up! They'd buy the album!" Mike said "I don't think I'll sell ten of these, but you guys are so passionate about it. I'll put up twenty-two thousand dollars. Go make the record."

Mr. Stewart told me later in 2002 (he was a major publishing mogul by then), when I was remastering the *Circle* for CD (with four extra cuts!) that it was one of three albums he had on his office wall. Two other albums he made happen (he was responsible for hundreds) were on his wall: *Imagine* by John Lennon and Tina Turner's first solo record after leaving Ike. It was excellent company.

We left and crossed the street to celebrate with pancakes and stuff at the IHOP. We were jubilant, happy . . . a record on the charts, and a budget to record an album with Earl, Travis, and Doc, and the others . . . and who else? I could not wait to tell the rest of the band what was coming. We weren't sure what it would be, but it would be good. By then (week 3, after asking Doc, Earl, and Travis—and Earl had just confirmed Maybelle) we were going to meet Roy Acuff the next month in Nashville. We were heading into learn fifteen new songs for this album, we thought. Then as it grew to thirty-six, we had to get more ready! What started as a double album would in a couple of months be a triple album—quite unheard of at that time.

Eight weeks after I asked Earl and Doc, we were in the studio, but first there were about twenty-two dates on the road on the way there. Bill had enlisted the engineer, Dino Lappas, with whom we did *Uncle Charlie* (and *Rare Junk,* our fourth album), and Dino booked Nashville's Woodland Sound Studios, one every Nashville musician knew of and would be comfortable with. We were on our way. . . to Nashville to make a record!

IN MEMORIAM

For all those who were there for creating the *Circle* and others who are part of the *Circle* family and have gone on to that "home in the sky."

William E. "Bill" McEuen, 1941–2020

Mother Maybelle Carter, 1909–1978

Earl Scruggs, 1924–2012

Randy Scruggs, 1953–2018

Louise Scruggs, 1927–2006

Doc Watson, 1923–2012

Roy Acuff, 1903–1992

Merle Travis, 1917–1983

Jimmy Martin, 1927–2005

Vassar Clements, 1928–2005

Roy "Junior" Huskey, 1928–1971

Pete "Bashful Brother Oswald" Kirby, 1911–2002

Jerry Jeff Walker, 1942–2020

John Prine, 1946–2020

Gary Scruggs, 1949–2021

THE *CIRCLE* FAMILY

Not many albums out there go on to have multiple volumes. Although the original *Circle* album stands on its own for creating magic from the original sessions, there are subsequent *Circle* albums, *Volume II* (1989), *Volume III* (2002), and *Circlin' Back: Celebrating 50 Years of the Nitty Gritty Dirt Band* (2016)—a live performance at Nashville's Ryman Auditorium recorded as a DVD/CD, that all have the title song "Will the Circle Be Unbroken" as the common connection, along with, of course, the Nitty Gritty Dirt Band. The three volumes each include a different rendition of "Will the Circle Be Unbroken" and end with an instrumental, "Both Sides Now," "Amazing Grace," and "Farther Along."

Circle Volume II featured a largely acoustic bluegrass selection of songs performed by artists from country, folk, rock, and pop music that included people who had become friends over the years: John Denver, Levon Helm, Johnny Cash, Emmylou Harris, Rosanne Cash, Michael Martin Murphey, Chris Hillman, Roger McGuinn, John Hiatt, John Prine, and Roy Huskey Jr. (son of Junior Huskey, who played on the original *Circle*). Also appearing from the original *Circle* album were Earl Scruggs, Jimmy Martin, Vassar Clements, Bashful Brother Oswald, and Roy Acuff. A number of other Nashville cats, session musicians, included Chet Atkins on guitar, Mark O'Connor on fiddle, Jerry Douglas on Dobro, Béla Fleck on banjo, and Tony Rice on guitar.

The album won three Grammy Awards in 1990, including Best Bluegrass Recording (for "The Valley Road" with Bruce Hornsby), Best Country Music Performance by a Duo or Group with Vocal, and Best Country Instrumental for "Amazing Grace" performed by Randy Scruggs. It also won Album of the Year at the Country Music Association Awards.

Circle Volume III was released in 2002 on the 30th anniversary of the original *Circle* album and would continue in the tradition of featuring bluegrass and traditional country music songs. Original *Circle* performers returning for *Volume III* included Earl Scruggs, Jimmy Martin, Doc Watson, Vassar Clements, and Randy Scruggs along with the Nitty Gritty Dirt Band. Randy Scruggs was the producer on both *Circle* Volumes II and III. Johnny Cash, Ricky Skaggs, and Emmylou Harris would also return from *Circle Volume II*. It featured a star-studded lineup that included Josh Graves, Rodney Dillard, Del McCoury, Taj Mahal, Willie Nelson, Tom Petty, Vince Gill, Dwight Yoakam, Iris Dement, June Carter Cash, Alison Kraus, and Matraca Berg. The album also included Jaime Hanna and Jonathan McEuen, sons of NGDB members Jeff Hanna and John McEuen; they performed "The Lowlands" (written by Gary Scruggs) with Jeff and John (and NGDB) accompanying their sons on guitar and banjo. There was also a DVD produced, *Will the Circle Be*

Unbroken—Farther Along with some extras, behind-the-scenes making of *Circle III*, extra songs from the live concert, and a video of "The Lowlands."

Circlin' Back Celebrating 50 years of the Nitty Gritty Dirt Band was recorded live in 2016 at the Ryman Auditorium and would be released as PBS special on DVD/CD. Although it celebrated fifty years of the NGDB, it was also a celebration of the *Circle* album and featured a number of songs from the previous *Circle* albums, including "My Walkin' Shoes," "Nine Pound Hammer," "Keep on the Sunny Side," and ended with "Will the Circle Be Unbroken." Among the many notable performances were Jerry Jeff Walker performing "Mr. Bojangles," John Prine with "Grandpa Was a Carpenter" and "Paradise," and with Vince Gill singing "Tennessee Stud."

The original *Circle* album has collected numerous honors including the Grammy Hall of Fame, the Library of Congress National Recording Registry, Grammy nomination for cover, and has multiple gold and platinum awards. It continues to be a top-selling bluegrass album on Amazon.

Some interesting trivia on the song, "Will the Circle Be Unbroken." The first documented recording of the song was in 1911 performed by William McEwan with a complete orchestra backing him—hmm, sixty years later, in 1971 the song/album would be produced by William E. McEuen—coincidence or meant to be?

Also known as "Can the Circle Be Unbroken," there have been 229 documented recordings of the song, either with the version credited to Charles H. Gabriel and Ada Habershon, or A. P. Carter. The Carter Family with A. P., Sarah, and Maybelle Carter would record their version "Can the Circle Be Unbroken" in 1935.

Among the 229 documented recordings, "Circle" has been recorded by Rose Maddox, Pat Boone, Earl Scruggs Revue, Doc Watson, June Carter Cash, Chet Atkins, Roy Acuff, the Staples Singers, George Jones, Ramblin' Jack Elliott, Joan Baez, Ronnie Hawkins, Delaney and Bonnie and Friends, Willie Nelson, Jimmy Martin, Jerry Jeff Walker, Arlo Guthrie and Pete Seeger, the Neville Brothers, Randy Travis, Richie Havens, and more.

The *Circle* also is a family affair where sons and daughters of performers on the original *Circle* album would appear in *Volumes II* and *III*, with Roy Huskey Jr., Ray Martin, Jaime Hanna, Jonathan McEuen, June Carter Cash, Richard Watson, and Gary and Randy Scruggs.

The "Circle" is sung every year at the Country Music Hall of Fame, at the conclusion of each medallion induction ceremony. It is performed by the inductees of that respective year as well as any previously inducted members of the Hall of Fame who are present.

Neil Young joined Bob Dylan on stage to play guitar and sing "Will the Circle Be Unbroken" together in July 2019 at Nowlan Park Stadium in Kilkenny, Ireland. Bob Dylan and the Band recorded a version of "Circle" on *The Bootleg Series Vol. 11 The Basement Tapes Complete* (2014). In 1971 Leon Russell would open his recording sessions at Homewood Studio with "Circle" as musicians entered.

Ken Burns *Country Music* documentary first aired in September 2019, an eight-part series that included episode 6 titled "Will the Circle Be Unbroken," covering the time period 1968–1972. With narration by Peter Coyote, episode 6 included interviews with John McEuen and other musicians sharing their stories of the recording session and their relationship to the "Circle" song. Dayton Duncan and Ken Burns also wrote and produced the book, *Country Music; An Illustrated History* based on the series that also included numerous references to the *Circle* sessions and album. The series final song was "Circle" as performed at Johnny Cash's funeral service.

Recommended Reading

Country Music: An Illustrated History. Based on the film series by Ken Burns and Dayton Duncan (Knopf, 2019). ISBN: 978-0-525-52054-2

DISCOGRAPHY

Track listing *Will the Circle Be Unbroken* (Original 1972) and *Circle 30th Anniversary* CD (2002) released by Capitol Records Nashville—a special vinyl-only edition was released in 2013 by Capitol Records Nashville

Disc One

"Grand Ole Opry Song" (Hylo Brown)—2:59

Jimmy Martin—lead vocal and guitar, John McEuen—banjo, Vassar Clements—fiddle, Les Thompson—mandolin, Roy "Junior" Huskey—bass, Jeff Hanna, Gary Scruggs, Jim Ibbotson, Thompson, and Ray Martin—background vocals

"Keep on the Sunny Side" (A. P. Carter, Gary Garett)—3:35

Mother Maybelle Carter—lead vocal and guitar, Doc Watson—guitar, Pete "Oswald" Kirby—Dobro, Roy "Junior" Huskey—bass, Earl Scruggs—banjo, Randy Scruggs—autoharp, McEuen—mandolin; Jeff Hanna, Les Thompson, Merle Travis, Jim Ibbotson, Doc Watson, and Gary Scruggs—background vocals.

"Nashville Blues" (Earl Scruggs)—3:10

Earl Scruggs—lead banjo, John McEuen—banjo, Jeff Hanna—washboard, Jimmie Fadden—harmonica, Vassar Clements—fiddle, Randy Scruggs—guitar, Norman Blake—Dobro, Roy "Junior" Huskey—bass

"You Are My Flower" (A. P. Carter)—3:35

Jeff Hanna, Gary Scruggs—lead vocals, Earl Scruggs—guitar, John McEuen—banjo, Norman Blake—Dobro, Jimmie Fadden—autoharp, Jim Ibbotson—snare, Roy "Junior" Huskey—bass, Randy Scruggs—guitar; Les Thompson—background vocals

"The Precious Jewel" (Roy Acuff)—3:30

Roy Acuff—lead vocal, John McEuen—banjo, Jimmie Fadden—harmonica, Les Thompson—mandolin, Earl Scruggs—guitar, Randy Scruggs—autoharp, Vassar Clements—fiddle, Roy "Junior" Huskey—bass, Pete "Oswald" Kirby—Dobro

"Dark as a Dungeon" (Merle Travis)—2:45

Merle Travis—lead vocal and guitar, John McEuen—mandolin, Jimmie Fadden—harmonica, Roy "Junior" Huskey—bass; Jeff Hanna, Les Thompson, and Jim Ibbotson—background vocals

"Tennessee Stud" (Jimmie Driftwood)—4:22

Doc Watson—lead vocal and guitar, John McEuen—banjo, Jimmie Fadden—harmonica, Jim Ibbotson—guitar, Roy "Junior" Huskey—bass, Vassar Clements—fiddle, Jeff Hanna—background vocal

"Black Mountain Rag" (traditional; credited to Thomas Magness on the album)—2:10

Doc Watson—lead guitar, John McEuen—banjo, Jim Ibbotson—guitar, Les Thompson—mandolin, Jimmie Fadden—harmonica, Vassar Clements—fiddle, Roy "Junior" Huskey—bass

"Wreck on the Highway" (Dorsey Dixon)—3:24

Roy Acuff—lead vocal, Jimmie Fadden—harmonica, Les Thompson—mandolin, Pete "Oswald" Kirby—Dobro, Earl Scruggs—guitar, Vassar Clements—fiddle, Roy "Junior" Huskey—bass

"The End of the World" (Fred Rose)—3:53

Pete "Oswald" Kirby—Dobro, Doc Watson—guitar, Earl Scruggs—guitar, Roy "Junior" Huskey—bass

"I Saw the Light" (Hank Williams)—3:45

Roy Acuff—lead vocal, Earl Scruggs—banjo, Jimmie Fadden—harmonica, John McEuen—mandolin, Doc Watson—guitar, Pete "Oswald" Kirby—Dobro, Vassar Clements—fiddle, Randy Scruggs—autoharp, Roy "Junior" Huskey—bass; Jeff Hanna, Les Thompson, Jim Ibbotson, and Jimmy Martin—background vocals

"Sunny Side of the Mountain" (Byron Gregory, Harry McAuliffe)—2:14

Jimmy Martin—lead vocal and guitar, John McEuen—banjo, Les Thompson—mandolin, Jimmie Fadden—harmonica, Jim Ibbotson—snare, Vassar Clements—fiddle, Roy "Junior" Huskey—bass; Jeff Hanna, Les Thompson, Gary Scruggs, and Ray Martin—background vocals

"Nine Pound Hammer" (Merle Travis)—2:14

Merle Travis—lead vocal and guitar, John McEuen—banjo, Jimmie Fadden—harmonica, Jim Ibbotson—snare, Roy "Junior" Huskey—bass; Jeff Hanna, Jim Ibbotson, and Les Thompson—background vocals

"Losin' You (Might Be the Best Thing Yet)" (Edria A. Humphrey, Jimmy Martin)—2:44

Jimmy Martin—lead vocal and guitar, John McEuen—banjo, Jimmie Fadden—harmonica, Les Thompson—mandolin, Jim Ibbotson—snare, Vassar Clements—fiddle, Roy "Junior" Huskey—bass

"Honky Tonkin'" (Hank Williams)—2:19

Jimmie Fadden—lead vocal, Jeff Hanna—guitar, Norman Blake—Dobro, Vassar Clements—lead guitar and fiddle, Les Thompson—mandolin, Roy "Junior" Huskey—bass, Jim Ibbotson—drums

"You Don't Know My Mind" (Jimmie Skinner)—2:45

Jimmy Martin—lead vocal and guitar, John McEuen—banjo, Les Thompson—mandolin, Jimmie Fadden—harmonica, Jim Ibbotson—drums, Roy "Junior" Huskey—bass, Vassar Clements—fiddle, Jeff Hanna, Les Thompson, Gary Scruggs, and Ray Martin—background vocals

"My Walkin' Shoes" (Jimmy Martin, Paul Williams)—2:02

Jimmy Martin—lead vocal and guitar, John McEuen—banjo, Les Thompson—mandolin, Jimmie Fadden—harmonica, Jim Ibbotson—snare, Vassar Clements—fiddle, Roy "Junior" Huskey—bass, Jeff Hanna, Les Thompson, Gary Scruggs, and Ray Martin—background vocals

Disc Two

"Lonesome Fiddle Blues" (Vassar Clements)—2:41

Vassar Clements—fiddle, John McEuen—banjo, Jim Ibbotson—guitar, Jimmie Fadden—harmonica, Jeff Hanna—washboard, Les Thompson—mandolin, Randy Scruggs—guitar, Ellis Padget—bass

"Cannonball Rag" (Merle Travis)—1:15

Merle Travis—guitar, Junior "Roy" Huskey—bass

"Avalanche" (Millie Clements)—2:50

Vassar Clements—fiddle, John McEuen—banjo, Jim Ibbotson—guitar, Jeff Hanna—washboard, Les Thompson—mandolin, Jimmie Fadden—harmonica, Roy "Junior" Huskey—bass

"Flint Hill Special" (Earl Scruggs)—2:12

Earl Scruggs—banjo, Jimmie Fadden—harmonica, Les Thompson—mandolin, Randy Scruggs—guitar, Norman Blake—Dobro, Vassar Clements—fiddle, Jim Ibbotson—snare, Roy "Junior" Huskey—bass

"Togary Mountain" (Walter McEuen)—2:25

John McEuen—banjo, Jim Ibbotson—guitar, Les Thompson—mandolin, Norman Blake—Dobro, Vassar Clements—fiddle, Roy "Junior" Huskey—bass

"Earl's Breakdown" (Earl Scruggs)—2:34

Earl Scruggs—banjo, Randy Scruggs—guitar, Vassar Clements—fiddle, Les Thompson—mandolin, Jim Ibbotson—snare, Roy "Junior" Huskey—bass

"Orange Blossom Special" (Ervin T. Rouse)—2:14

Vassar Clements—fiddle, John McEuen—banjo, Les Thompson—mandolin, Jimmie Martin—guitar, Jim Ibbotson—snare, Randy Scruggs—guitar, Ellis Padgett—bass

"Wabash Cannonball" (A. P. Carter)—2:00

Pete "Oswald" Kirby—Dobro, Jimmie Fadden—harmonica, Doc Watson—guitar, Roy "Junior" Huskey—bass, Earl Scruggs—guitar

"Lost Highway" (Leon Payne)—3:37

Jim Ibbotson—lead vocal and guitar, Les Thompson—mandolin, Jeff Hanna—drums, Vassar Clements—fiddle, Pete "Oswald" Blake—Dobro, Roy "Junior" Huskey—bass, John McEuen—banjo

Doc Watson and Merle Travis First Meeting (Dialogue)—1:52

"Way Downtown" (traditional, Doc Watson)—3:30

Doc Watson—lead vocal and guitar, John McEuen—banjo, Les Thompson—mandolin, Jim Ibbotson—guitar, Jimmie Fadden—harmonica, Vassar Clements—fiddle, Roy "Junior" Huskey—bass, Jeff Hanna—background vocal

"Down Yonder" (arranged by Doc Watson)—1:48

Doc Watson—guitar, John McEuen—banjo, Jim Ibbotson—guitar, Jimmie Fadden—harmonica, Les Thompson—mandolin, Jeff Hanna—washboard, Vassar Clements—fiddle, Roy "Junior" Huskey—bass

"Pins and Needles (in My Heart)" (Floyd Jenkins)—2:53

Roy Acuff—lead vocal, Pete "Oswald" Kirby—Dobro, Jimmie Fadden—harmonica, Les Thompson—mandolin, John McEuen—banjo, Earl Scruggs—guitar, Vassar Clements—fiddle, Jim Ibbotson—snare, Roy "Junior" Huskey—bass

"Honky Tonk Blues" (Hank Williams)—2:22

Jeff Hanna—lead vocal, Bill McEuen—guitar, Jim Ibbotson—drums, Pete "Oswald" Blake—Dobro, Vassar Clements—fiddle, Roy "Junior" Huskey—bass

"Sailin' on to Hawaii" (Beecher Kirby)—2:00

Pete "Oswald" Kirby—Dobro, Doc Watson—guitar, Scruggs—guitar, Roy "Junior" Huskey—bass

"I'm Thinking Tonight of My Blue Eyes" (A. P. Carter)—4:25

Maybelle Carter—lead vocal and guitar, Earl Scruggs—banjo, John McEuen—mandolin, Merle Travis—guitar, Pete "Oswald" Kirby—Dobro, Vassar Clements—fiddle, Roy "Junior" Huskey—bass, Jeff Hanna, Les Thompson, Jim Ibbotson, and Randy Scruggs—background vocals

"I Am a Pilgrim" (traditional)—2:55

Merle Travis—lead vocal and guitar, Jimmie Fadden—harmonica, Jim Ibbotson—snare, Roy "Junior" Huskey—bass

"Wildwood Flower" (A. P. Carter)—3:34

Maybelle Carter—lead vocal and autoharp, Earl Scruggs—guitar, Jim Ibbotson—guitar, Les Thompson—mandolin, Roy "Junior" Huskey—bass

"Soldier's Joy" (John McEuen, Earl Scruggs)—2:05

Earl Scruggs—banjo, John McEuen—Uncle Dave Macon's banjo, Roy "Junior" Huskey—bass

"Will the Circle Be Unbroken" (A. P. Carter)—4:50

Maybelle Carter—lead vocal (first and fourth verses) and autoharp, Earl Scruggs—banjo, Doc Watson—guitar, Chet Atkins—guitar, Jimmie Fadden—harmonica, Merle Travis—guitar, John McEuen—mandolin, Jimmie Martin—lead vocal (second verse) and guitar, Pete "Oswald" Kirby—Dobro, Vassar Clements—fiddle, Roy "Junior" Huskey—bass, Roy Acuff—lead vocal (third verse), Doc Watson, Jeff Hanna, Jim Ibbotson, Les Thompson, Gary Scruggs, Ray Martin, Timmy Martin, Randy Scruggs, Betty Travis, Fred Cross, Gloria Belle, Louise Scruggs, Steve Scruggs, Chet Flippo, Martha Flippo, Larry Murray, Mike Carr, and Alice McEuen—background vocals

"Both Sides Now" (Joni Mitchell)—2:19

Randy Scruggs—guitar

2002 Reissue bonus tracks

"Foggy Mountain Breakdown" (Earl Scruggs)—2:39

Warming Up for "The Opry"—2:43

Sunny Side—4:06

"Remember Me" (Scotty Wiseman)—1:32

Track Listing *Will The Circle Be Unbroken Vol. 2* Released By MCA Nashville

"Life's Railway to Heaven" (Traditional, arranged by Johnny Cash)—4:39

lead vocal and guitar by Johnny Cash with June Carter Cash, Anita Carter, and Helen Carter (as the Carter Family)

Randy Scruggs plays "Mother" Maybelle Carter's Gibson L5

"Grandpa Was a Carpenter" (John Prine)—3:24

lead vocal and guitar by John Prine

"When I Get My Rewards" (Paul Kennerley)—4:25

lead vocal by Levon Helm

"Don't You Hear Jerusalem Moan" (Traditional)—3:56

mandolin and first verse lead vocals by Sam Bush, second verse vocals by Bob Carpenter and John Cowan, third verse vocals by Jimmy Ibbotson and Pat Flynn

"Little Mountain Church House (Jim Rushing, Carl Jackson)—3:32

lead vocal and guitar by Ricky Skaggs

"And So It Goes" (Paul Overstreet, Don Schlitz)—3:54

lead vocal by John Denver

Released on John Denver's Australian album *Stonehaven Sunset*

"When It's Gone" (Jimmie Fadden, Don Schlitz)—2:34

lead vocal by Jimmy Ibbotson

"Mary Danced with Soldiers" (Kennerley)—3:07

lead vocal and guitar by Emmylou Harris

"Riding Alone" (Bob Carpenter, Jeff Hanna, Richard Hathaway)—3:09

lead vocals by Bob Carpenter and Emmylou Harris

"I'm Sitting on Top of the World" (Lonnie Chatmon, Walter Vinson)—3:10

lead vocal and guitar by Jimmy Martin

"Lovin' on the Side" (Paulette Carlson, Jimmy Ibbotson, Sandy Waltner)—2:57

lead vocal by Paulette Carlson

"Lost River" (Michael Martin Murphey)—3:26

lead vocal and guitar by Michael Martin Murphey

"Bayou Jubilee" (Jeff Hanna)—3:01

lead vocal by Jeff Hanna

"Blues Berry Hill" (Bob Carpenter, Jimmie Fadden, Jeff Hanna, Jimmy Ibbotson, Randy Scruggs)—3:26

instrumental, featuring Randy Scruggs on lead guitar

"Turn of the Century" (J. Fred Knobloch, Dan Tyler)—3:39

lead vocals by Jimmy Ibbotson (first verse), Jeff Hanna (second verse), and Bob Carpenter (third verse)

"One Step Over the Line" (John Hiatt)—4:30

lead vocal and guitar by John Hiatt with Rosanne Cash, vocals

"You Ain't Goin' Nowhere" (Bob Dylan)—3:53

lead vocals and twelve-string guitar by Roger McGuinn with Chris Hillman, lead vocals and guitar

"The Valley Road" (Bruce Hornsby)—4:13

lead vocals and piano by Bruce Hornsby

"Will the Circle Be Unbroken" (A. P. Carter/last verse lyrics by Jimmy Ibbotson)—5:39

lead vocals by Johnny Cash (first verse), Roy Acuff (second verse), Ricky Skaggs (third verse), Levon Helm, with Emmylou Harris (fourth verse) and Jimmy Ibbotson (fifth verse); backing choir: Roy Acuff, Cynthia Biederman, Sam Bush, Paulette Carlson, Bob Carpenter, Gretchen Carpenter, June Carter Cash, Johnny Cash, Cindy Cash, Rosanne Cash, John Cowan, Steve Dahl, John Denver, Jimmie Fadden, Béla Fleck, Pat Flynn, Radney Foster, Vince Gill, Jeff Hanna, Melody Hanna, John Hiatt, Chris Hillman, Bruce Hornsby, Jimmy Ibbotson, Helen Carter Jones, David Jones, Bashful Brother Oswald, Bill Lloyd, Jimmy Martin, Michael Martin Murphey, Roger McGuinn, Tracy Nelson, Robert Oermann, Brad Parker, Don Schlitz, Earl Scruggs, Gary Scruggs, Randy Scruggs, Steve Scruggs, Lynn Shults, Marty Stuart, Wendy Waldman, Steve Wariner, Cheryl White, Sharon White, and Bobbie White

"Amazing Grace" (John Newton)—1:48

Solo guitar, performed by Randy Scruggs

Track listing *Will the Circle Be Unbroken Vol. 3*
Released 2002 by Capitol Records Nashville

Disc 1

"Take Me in Your Lifeboat" (Traditional)—3:42

"Milk Cow Blues" (Kokomo Arnold)—5:03

"I Find Jesus" (Jimmy Ibbotson)—3:52

"Hold Whatcha Got" (Jimmy Martin)—2:55

"Mama's Opry" (Iris DeMent)—4:21

"Diamonds in the Rough" (A. P. Carter, Maybelle Carter, Sara Carter)—3:39

"Lonesome River" (Carter Stanley)—4:23

"Some Dark Holler" (Traditional)—3:19

"The Lowlands" (Gary Scruggs)—3:49

"Love, Please Come Home" (Leon Jackson)—2:48

"Goodnight Irene" (Huddie Ledbetter, John A. Lomax)—3:54

"I Know What It Means to be Lonesome" (James Brockman, James Kendis, Nathaniel Vincent)—3:49

"I'll Be Faithful to You" (Paul Kennerley)—2:32

"Tears in the Holston River" (John R. Cash)—4:14

Disc 2

"Fishin' Blues" (Traditional)—4:31

"Save It, Save It" (Charles Rufus Shoffner)—1:57

"Wheels" (Chris Hillman, Gram Parsons)—3:14

"Roll in My Sweet Baby's Arms" (Traditional)—3:53

"Oh Cumberland" (Matraca Berg, Gary Harrison)—4:21

"I Am a Pilgrim" (Traditional)—4:09

"Sallie Ann" (Earl Scruggs)—2:37

"Catfish John" (Bob McDill, Alan Reynolds)—4:07

"Roll the Stone Away" (Jeff Hanna, Marcus Hummon)—4:09

"All Prayed Up" (Vince Gill)—3:09

"Return to Dismal Swamp II" (Walter McEuen, William McEuen)—3:16

"There Is a Time" (Mitchell Jayne, Rodney Dillard)—3:31

"Will the Circle Be Unbroken/Glory, Glory" (A. P. Carter, Traditional)—4:39

"Farther Along" (Traditional)—1:10

Enhanced CD Extras

Disc 2 also contains a behind-the-scenes video of the song "Take Me in Your Lifeboat."

Personnel

Bob Carpenter—harmony vocal, accordion

Jimmie Fadden—harmonica, snare, harmony vocal

Jeff Hanna—lead and harmony vocal, guitar, mandolin, National slide guitar, washboard

Jimmy Ibbotson—lead and harmony vocal, snare, percussion box, guitar, bouzouki, drum box, kick drum, porch board

John McEuen—banjo, mandolin, frailing banjo, finger-style lead guitar, harmony vocal

Featured lead vocalists

Matraca Berg—lead vocal, harmony vocal, guitar

Sam Bush—lead vocal, mandolin

June Carter Cash—lead vocal, autoharp

Johnny Cash—lead vocal, guitar

Iris DeMent—lead vocal, guitar

Rodney Dillard—lead vocal, guitar

Pat Enright—lead vocal, guitar

Vince Gill—lead vocal, guitar

Jaime Hanna—lead vocal, guitar, sticks

Emmylou Harris—lead vocal, guitar, harmony vocal

Alison Krauss—lead vocal, fiddle

Taj Mahal—lead vocal, archtop guitar

Jimmy Martin—lead vocal, guitar

Del McCoury—lead vocal, guitar

Jonathan McEuen—lead vocal, guitar

Willie Nelson—lead vocal, guitar

Tom Petty—lead vocal, guitar

Randy Scruggs—lead vocal, guitar, banjo, mandolin

Ricky Skaggs—lead vocal, mandolin

Doc Watson—lead vocal, guitar

Dwight Yoakam—lead vocal, guitar

Special guest musicians

Barry Bales—upright bass

Vassar Clements—fiddle

Mike Compton—mandolin

Dennis Crouch—upright bass

Jerry Douglas—Dobro

Dan Dugmore—Dobro

Glen Duncan—fiddle

Stuart Duncan—fiddle

Kevin Grantt—upright bass

Josh Graves—Dobro

Byron House—upright bass

David Jackson—upright bass

Ray Martin—harmony vocal, mandolin

Robbie McCoury—banjo

Ronnie McCoury—mandolin

David Nance—harmony vocal, Dobro

Alan O'Brant—banjo

Mickey Raphael—harmonica

Tony Rice—lead guitar

Earl Scruggs—banjo

Richard Watson—guitar

Glenn Worf—upright bass

The Nitty Gritty Dirt Band, *Circlin' Back, Celebrating 50 Years*, recorded live at Ryman Auditorium 2016. Directed by Gary Scruggs, Music Director Jeff Hanna. (CD/DVD, NGDB Record, Aired on PBS)

1. You Ain't Going Nowhere
2. Grandpa Was a Carpenter *featuring John Prine*
3. Paradise *featuring John Prine*
4. My Walkin' Shoes
5. Tennessee Stud *featuring Vince Gill*
6. Nine Pound Hammer *featuring Sam Bush and Vince Gill*
7. Buy for Me the Rain
8. These Days *featuring Jackson Browne*
9. Truthful Parson Brown *featuring Jackson Browne, Byron House, Jerry Douglas, and Sam Bush*

10. Keep on the Sunny Side *featuring Alison Krauss*

11. Catfish John *featuring Alison Krauss*

12. An American Dream *featuring Alison Krauss and Rodney Crowell*

13. Long Hard Road (Sharecropper's Dream) *featuring Rodney Crowell*

14. Mr. Bojangles *featuring Jerry Jeff Walker*

15. Fishing in the Dark *featuring Jimmy Ibbotson*

16. Bayou Jubilee/Sally Was a Goodun'

17. Jambalaya

18. Will the Circle Be Unbroken

Featured performers: five-string banjo, mandolin, fiddle, lap steel guitar, acoustic guitar—John McEuen; bass, electric bass—Byron House (track 9); Dobro, lap steel guitar—Jerry Douglas (track 9); vocals, acoustic guitar—Jerry Jeff Walker (track 14); Jimmy Ibbotson (tracks 15, 16); John Prine (tracks 2, 3); Rodney Crowell (tracks 12, 13); Vince Gill (tracks 5, 6); vocals, acoustic guitar, electric guitar—Jackson Browne (tracks 8, 9); vocals, acoustic guitar, electric guitar, washboard—Jeff Hanna; vocals, drums, harmonica—Jimmie Fadden; vocals, fiddle—Alison Krauss (tracks 10, 11, 12); vocals, keyboards, accordion—Bob Carpenter (track 2); vocals, mandolin, fiddle—Sam Bush (tracks 5, 9).

Discography for John McEuen and Nitty Gritty Dirt Band

John McEuen (Warner Bros., 1986)

String Wizards (Vanguard Records, 1991)

John McEuen and the LA String Wizards, *Round Trip—Live in LA 2005*

Stories & Songs with Jimmy Ibbotson (Planetary Records, 2000)

String Wizards II (Grammy nominated; Vanguard Records, 1996)

acoustic Traveller (Vanguard Records, 1997)

The Music of the Wild West (Western Heritage Award; Varese/Saraband, 1999)

Chief Jim Billie, *Alligator Tales* (SOAR Records, 1998)

String Wizard's Picks (best of) enhanced with video (Vanguard Records, 1998)

Round Trip, Live (Rural Rhythm, 2007)

Nitty Gritty Surround DVD (AIX Records, 2001)

Vanguard Visionaries (Vanguard Records, 2007)

Kids Favorite Country Songs (Sesame Street, 2010)

The McEuen Sessions: For All the Good, with sons Jonathan and Nathan (Mesa Bluemoon, 2012)

Made in Brooklyn (winner Americana award; Chesky Records, 2016)

"The Dogs Are in the Woods," *Johnny Cash Forever Words* (Sony Legacy Music, 2020)

"The Nashville Sessions" (Digital—streaming download, 2021)

Additional Songs and Albums Featuring John McEuen

Steve Martin, *The Crow; New Songs for the Five-String Banjo* (Grammy Best Bluegrass Album)

The Steve Martin Brothers, 1981

Marshall Tucker Band, *Long Hard Ride*

Michael Martin Murphey songs "Carolina in the Pines," "Wildfire," and four albums

Mike Maki (1974)

David Allan Coe, "Just Divorced" (1984)

Timberline, "Circlin," *The Great Timber Rush* (1977)

Vassar Clements, *Vassar Clements* (1975)

Hoyt Axton, "Gotta Keep Rollin," *A Rusty Old Halo* (1979)

The Amazing Rhythm Aces, *Full House/Aces High* (1981)

Tribute to Steve Goodman, "Face on the Cutting Room Floor" (1985)

Earl Scruggs, *I Saw the Light with Some Help from My Friends* (2005)

Phish, "Amazing Grace," "I Want to Be a Cowboy Sweetheart," *Vegas 96* and *Road to Vegas*

Nathan McEuen, *Scrapbook Sessions* (2010)

Bill Wyman, *Monkey Grip* (1974)

David Bromberg, "The Fields Turned Brown," *Only Slightly Mad* (2013)

Other performances from John McEuen

"The Cremation of Sam McGee," internet 2022

"The Newsman," internet 2021

Music Videos

"Return to Dismal Swamp" (Vanguard Records, 1992)

"Miner's Night Out" (Vanguard Records, 1993)

"Oh, Susanna" (Sesame Street, 2010)

Books

    The Life I've Picked (Chicago Review Press, 2018)

    The Mountain Whippoorwill (illustrated children's book, 2022)

Radio

    SiriusXM on the Village: *The Acoustic Traveller Show* since 2006

The Nitty Gritty Dirt Band Discography

The Nitty Gritty Dirt Band (Liberty, 1967)

Ricochet (Liberty, 1967)

Rare Junk (Liberty, 1968)

Alive! (Liberty, 1969)

Uncle Charlie & His Dog Teddy (Liberty, 1970)

All The Good Times (United Artists Records, 1971)

Will the Circle Be Unbroken (United Artists Records, 1972)

Stars and Stripes Forever (United Artists Records, 1974)

Symphonion Dream (United Artists Records, 1975)

Dirt Silver and Gold (United Artists Records, 1976)

The Dirt Band (United Artists Records, 1978)

An American Dream (United Artists Records, 1979)

Make a Little Magic (Liberty Records, 1980)

Jealousy (Liberty Records, 1981)

Let's Go (Liberty, 1982)

Plain Dirt Fashion (Warner Bros. Records, 1984)

Partners, Brothers and Friends (Warner Bros. Records, 1985)

Twenty Years of Dirt (Warner Bros. Records, 1986)

Hold On (Warner Bros. Records, 1987)

Workin' Band (Warner Bros. Records, 1988)

Will the Circle Be Unbroken Vol. II (Universal Records, 1989)

More Great Dirt (Warner Bros. Records, 1989)

The Rest of the Dream (MCA Records, 1990)

Live Two Five (Capitol Nashville, 1991)

Not Fade Away (Liberty Records, 1992)

acoustic (Liberty Records, 1994)

The Christmas Album (Rising Tide, 1997)

Bang Bang Bang (DreamWorks Records, 1998)

Will the Circle Be Unbroken, Volume III (Capitol Records, 2002)

Unbroken Live! (Delta Deluxe, 2003)

Welcome to Woody Creek (Blue Rose Records, 2004)

Speed of Life (Sugar Hill Records, 2009)

Circlin' Back, Celebrating 50 Years (NGDB Records, 2016)

INDEX

INDEX OF SONGS

PERFORMED ON THE *CIRCLE* ALBUM

OTHER SONGS OF NOTE AND INFLUENCE